POCKET MECHANIC
VOLVO

GW01465821

COVERING:

BY PETER RUSSEK

Published by
Peter Russek Publications Ltd.
Little Stone House, High Street,
Marlow/Bucks.

ISBN No. 0 - 903168 - 19 - 7

Library of Congress Catalogue Card No. 72 - 87386

The Publisher would like to thank Mr. R. Pickering for producing many of the illustrations in this Repair Guide.

Printed in England

PREFACE

Small though this guide is in size, it lacks no detail in covering the whole of the servicing and repair of the Volvo 140 series vehicles, from their introduction in 1967 right through to the 1973 models, for both carburettor and fuel injection engines. Brief, easy-to-follow instructions are given, free from unnecessary complication and repetition, yet containing all the necessary technical detail and information, and including over one hundred diagrams and illustrations.

Compiled and illustrated by experts, this guide provides a concise source of helpful information, all of which has been cross-checked for accuracy to the manufacturer's official service and repair procedures. Where special tools are required these are referred to, and identified, in the text and we do not hesitate to advise you if we feel that the operation cannot be properly undertaken without the use of such tools.

The reader's own judgement must ultimately decide just what work he will feel able to undertake but there is no doubt that, with this guide to assist him, there will be many more occasions where the delay, inconvenience and cost of garage repairs can be avoided or minimised.

This guide is produced in a handy glove-pocket size with the aim that it should always be kept in the vehicle whilst you are travelling. Many garage mechanics themselves use these publications in their work and if you have the book with you in the car you will have an invaluable source of reference which will quickly repay its modest initial cost.

We recommend that you remove the large Wiring Diagram from the pocket of the rear cover and pin it to your garage door or to another convenient place.

0. INTRODUCTION

0.0. General Information

This Repair Guide covers the Volvo 140 series of vehicles since their introduction in 1967. Originally marketed with the B18 A and B18 B engines of 1778 c.c. capacity, the series was up-rated in 1970 to the B20 A and B20 B engines of 1990 c.c. Electronically controlled fuel injection engines (B20 E and B20 F) were later introduced and are covered in this Repair Guide.

The Repair Guide is written and illustrated, in general, for the current (1973) models, with the necessary additional data and instructions for the earlier models.

It must, however, be pointed out that A B Volvo, the manufacturer of the vehicles, have a policy of making a more frequent revision to specifications and components than is usual for some other manufacturers. The vehicles are often introduced with new features at yearly intervals and, in addition, the engine accessories may change either in manufacturer or type according to the year of the vehicle or the market for which it has been produced.

It is, therefore, essential that spares or replacements are always obtained for the particular model and year of the vehicle. Whilst we have given the information and data we consider of most value to the reader it is obvious that we cannot detail all changes occurring over the period of time that the range has been in production. We suggest that you obtain your spares and parts from an authorised Volvo dealer or distributor, providing him with the vehicle serial number and year of manufacture so that he can supply the correct parts for the vehicle in question.

0.1. Identification

The type designations of the Volvo 140 series of vehicles are as follows:

Two-door Saloon:	Type 142
Four-door Saloon:	Type 144
Estate car (Station Wagon):	Type 145

De Luxe and Grand Luxe versions are available and it should be noted that certain vehicles may have special features for the particular market for which they have been manufactured.

Identification plates and numbers are found as follows:

(1) Vehicle type designation; on a plate on the engine compartment rear bulkhead.

(2) Body number; on a separate plate on the bulkhead.

(3) Type designation and chassis number; on the front right-hand door pillar.

(4) Engine type, part number and serial number; on the left side of the engine block.

(5) Gearbox type, part number and serial number; on a plate fixed to the underside of the gearbox.

(6) Final drive, reduction ratio, part number and serial number; on a plate attached to the left-hand side of the casing.

0.2. Dimensions and Weights

Data given for models 142, 144 and 145.

Length:	*4630 mm (182.2 in.)*
Width:	*1705 mm (67 in.)*
Height:	
142 and 144:	*1442 mm (56.8 in.)*
145:	*1455 mm (57.3 in.)*
Wheelbase:	*2620 mm (103.3 in.)*
Ground clearance (unladen):	*210 mm (8.3 in.)*

Track — Front:	1350 mm (53.6 in.)
— Rear:	1350 mm (53.6 in.)
Turning circle:	9.6 m (31 ft. 6 in.)

Kerb Weight (approx.)	De Luxe	Grand Luxe
142:	1190 kg (2620 lb.)	1220 kg (2685 lb.)
144:	1210 kg (2665 lb.)	1245 kg (2740 lb.)
145:	1275 kg (2805 lb.)	1295 kg (2850 lb.)

NOTE: Weights given for current vehicles; earlier vehicles slightly different.

0.3.   General Servicing Notes

The servicing and repair instructions in this Repair Guide are laid out in an easy-to-follow step-by-step order and no difficulty should be encountered if the text and diagrams are followed carefully and methodically.

The "Technical Data" sections form an important part of the servicing and overhaul procedures and should always be referred to during work on the vehicle. In order that we can include as much data as possible you will find that we do not repeat in the text the values already given as technical data. For the same reason, we do not repeat each time the more obvious steps necessary to conform to good engineering practice. We, therefore, summarise below a few of the more important procedures and briefly draw your attention to some points of general interest.

Always use the torque settings given in the various sections of the Repair Guide. Bolts and nuts should be assembled in a clean and dry condition and the faces and threads should be free from damage, burrs or scoring.

All joint washers, gaskets, tab and lock washers, split pins and "O" rings must be renewed on assembly. Oil seals will, in the majority of cases, also need to be replaced if the seal and shaft have been separated. Connecting rod nuts and bolts should be replaced with new parts when the engine is serviced or dismantled.

References to left-hand and right-hand sides are always to be taken as if the observer is at the rear of the car, facing forward.

Always make quite sure that the car is adequately supported before commencing any work on the underside of the car. A small jack or make-shift prop can be highly dangerous and proper axle stands are an essential safety requirement.

Dirt, grease or mineral oil will rapidly destroy the seals of the hydraulic system and even the smallest amounts must be prevented from entering the system or coming into contact with the components. You are advised to read Section 8.3. before commencing any work on the brake hydraulic system.

Always obtain genuine manufacturer's spares and replacement parts. Cheaper alternative components may look the same but are not always to the same specification or quality.

Removal and installation instructions, in this Repair Guide, mean simply that instructions are given to take away from, or put back into, the vehicle the unit or part in question. Other instructions, usually headed "servicing", will cover the steps to completely dismantle or assemble a unit. Obviously, in some cases this may not be necessary or desirable and we recommend that units are not dismantled unless there is good reason to do so.

If the vehicle is fitted with any special features (exhaust emission control, fuel injection, air conditioning and so on) the reader is advised to study the appropriate sections before commencing any dismantling of the engine or other major units to see if there are any special precautions or steps that must be observed.

In the case of the two engines with fuel injection the main features and components are dealt with in the separate sections commencing at 13.0.

There is no reason why general engine overhaul should not be carried out for these engines but it is not recommended that the owner should attempt to dismantle or adjust any of the equipment for fuel injection or control.

1. ENGINE

1.0. Main Features

1.0.0. B18 ENGINES

Number of cylinders:	*4*
Arrangement:	*In line*
Valve gear:	*O.H.V.*

Identification:	
Year/Model:	*Engine/Compression Ratio:*
1967/144S:	*B18 A/10 : 1*
1967/144:	*B18 A/8.7 : 1*
1968-69/P142:	*B18 B/10 : 1*
1968-69/P144 and 145:	*B18 B/10 : 1*
1968-69/P142, 144, 145:	*B18 A/8.7 : 1*

Capacity (displacement):	*1778 c.c.*
Bore:	*84.14 mm (3.313 in.)*
Stroke:	*80 mm (3.150 in.)*

B.H.P. at rpm:	
B18 A (8.7 : 1 C/R):	*85 SAE at 5,000*
B18 B (10 : 1 C/R):	*115 SAE at 6,000*

Max. Torque, SAE:	
B18 A (8.7 : 1 C/R):	*15 kgm (108 lb.ft.) at 3,000 rpm*
B18 B (10 : 1 C/R):	*15.5 kgm (112 lb.ft.) at 4,000 rpm*

Compression Pressure (250 - 300 rpm):	
B18 A (8.7 : 1 C/R):	*11 - 13 kg/sq.cm (156 - 185 psi)*
B18 B:	*12 - 14 kg/sq.cm (170 - 200 psi)*

Engine weight (approx.):	*155 kg (341 lb.)*

Idling Speed:	
P142, 144, 145 (B18 A):	*500 - 700 rpm*
All others:	*600 - 800 rpm*

Firing order:	*1 - 3 - 4 - 2*

1.0.1. B20 A AND B20 B ENGINES

Number of cylinders:	*4*
Arrangement:	*In line*
Valve gear:	*O.H.V.*
Engine type:	*Carburettor (one or two)*
Capacity (displacement):	*1986 c.c.*
Bore:	*88.9 mm (3.50 in.)*
Stroke:	*80.0 mm (3.15 in.)*

B.H.P. at rpm:
  B20 A: 90 SAE at 4,800
  B20 B: 118 SAE at 5,800

Max. Torque, SAE:
  B20 A: 16.5 kgm (119 lb.ft.)
                                at 3,000
  B20 B: 17 kgm (124 lb.ft.)
                                at 3,500

Compression Ratio:
  B20 A: 8.7 : 1
  B20 B: 9.3 : 1

Compression Pressure (250 - 300 rpm):
  B20 A: 10 - 12 kg/sq.cm
                                (142 - 170 psi)
  B20 B: 11 - 13 kg/sq.cm
                                (156 - 185 psi)

Idling Speed:
  B20 A: 700 rpm
  B20 B: 800 rpm
  B20 B (with auto. transm.):   700 rpm

Firing order: 1 - 3 - 4 - 2

1.0.2.   B20 E AND B20 F ENGINES

Number of cylinders: 4
Arrangement: In line
Valve gear: O.H.V.
Engine type: Electronically controlled
                               fuel injection
Capacity (displacement):   1986 c.c.
Bore: 88.9 mm (3.50 in.)
Stroke: 80.0 mm (3.15 in.)

B.H.P. at rpm:
  B20 E: 135 SAE at 6,000
  B20 F: 112 SAE (J 245) at 6,000

Max. Torque, SAE:
  B20 E: 18 kgm (130 lb.ft.)
                               at 3,500
  B20 F (SAE J 245):   16 kgm (115 lb.ft.)
                               at 3,500

Compression Ratio:
  B20 E: 10.5 : 1
  B20 F: 8.7 : 1

Compression Pressure (250 - 300 rpm):
  B20 E: 12 - 14 kg/sq.cm
                               (170 - 200 psi)
  B20 F: 9 - 11 kg/sq.cm
                               (128 - 156 psi)

Firing order: 1 - 3 - 4 - 2

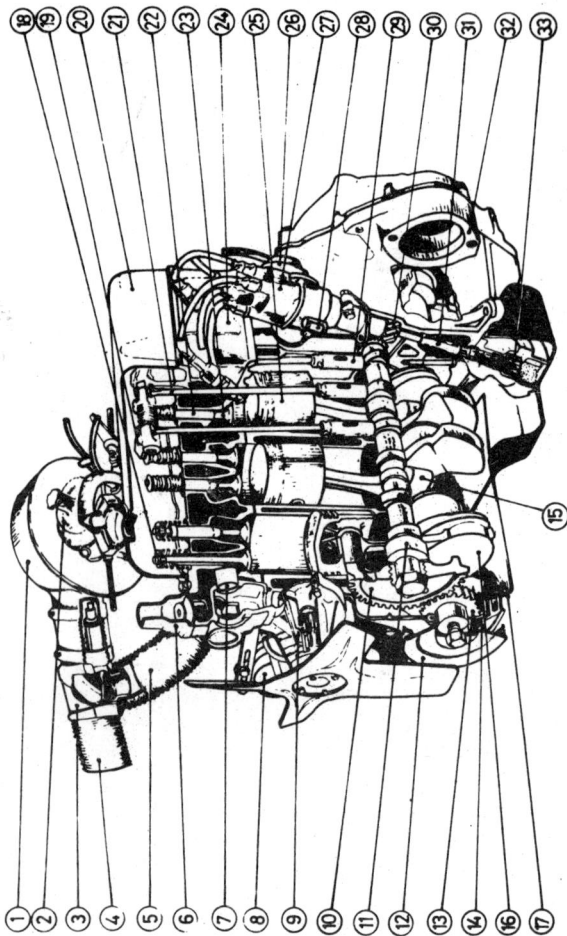

Fig. 1. – Section of the B 20 engine.

1. Air cleaner
2. Carburettor
3. Flap, constant air temperature device
4. Cold air hose
5. Hot air hose
6. Thermostat housing
7. Water distribution tube
8. Alternator
9. Water pump
10. Camshaft gear
11. Camshaft
12. Crankshaft pulley and bolt
13. Crankshaft gear
14. Timing drive cover
15. Connecting rod, big end cap and bearing
16. Crankshaft
17. Oil sump
18. Valve cap, collets and spring
19. Rocker arm
20. Rocker cover
21. Push rod
22. Valve guide
23. Valve
24. Cylinder head
25. Piston
26. Vacuum governor
27. Distributor
28. Capacitor
29. Tappet
30. Distributor drive
31. Oil pump drive shaft
32. Starter motor facing
33. Oil pump

1.1. Engine — Removal and Installation

1.1.0. REMOVAL — B18 A AND B AND B20 A AND B ENGINES

The engine and gearbox are removed together, with the engine auxiliaries left in position. The engine has to be lifted out at a fairly steep angle and the proper lifting equipment is recommended. Lifting attachment points are provided at the front and rear of the engine and if the proper equipment is not available it is suggested that extension plates are made up for attachment to the lifting positions.

Remove the gear lever from the car. Empty the cooling system and remove the bonnet (hood) from its hinges. Disconnect the battery positive lead. It is also a good precaution to remove the battery from the car.

Remove the distributor cap and leads and take off the low tension cable as well. Disconnect and remove the ignition coil. Take off the starter motor leads. Disconnect the fuel hoses from the pump and take off the air cleaner(s). Remove the alternator or dynamo leads and disconnect the temperature and oil pressure cables.

Remove the reverse (back-up) light cable and, if appropriate, the overdrive cable. Remove the pre-heating plate and the exhaust manifold nuts. Remove the throttle and choke wires. Take off the vacuum hose for the brake servo (at the manifold).

Disconnect the radiator hoses and remove the radiator. Drain the engine oil. Fit lifting arm SVO 2867 to the front of the engine and fit SVO 2870 to the rear of the engine.

Jack up under the engine and remove the lower nuts from the engine front mountings. Fit the engine hoist and beam (SVO 2810) to the lifting brackets.

Disconnect the clutch cable and spring from the clutch housing lever. Disconnect the engine earth (ground) cable and take out the speedometer cable from the gearbox. Remove the exhaust pipe clamp and the gearbox member.

Disconnect the propeller shaft from the gearbox end and secure it well out of the way.

Hoist the engine, at the same time lowering the rear end and raising the front. Pull the engine across the front of the car and lift it out carefully.

1.1.1.   REMOVAL – B20 E AND F ENGINES

The engine fitted with fuel injection is removed in a similar manner to the conventional engines, but these points must be followed:

Remove the pressure sensor hose from the inlet duct. Remove the fuel hose for the cold start valve and the fuel hoses at the bulkhead (firewall). Remove the plug contacts for the temperature sensor, the cold start valve and the throttle valve switch. Remove the hose for the induction air. Remove the ground lead from the inlet duct.

Remove the injectors carefully. Take off the bolts for the pressure regulator bracket and take out the injectors and fit protective plugs and masking tape. Place the injectors, distributing pipe and pressure regulator to one side and secure in position.

Remove the plug contact and lead from the distributor. Lift out the engine with the hoist as before.

IMPORTANT!   Take great care not to damage or contaminate the fuel injectors or fuel system.

1.1.2.   INSTALLATION – B18 A AND B AND B20 A AND B ENGINES

Install the engine and gearbox into the engine compartment with the same hoist and attachments as for removal. Install the speedometer cable and the propeller shaft after having seated the engine onto the mountings.

Secure the exhaust manifold together with the gasket and pre-heater plate. Fit the clutch cable and adjust the clutch. Fit the exhaust manifold clamp. Connect the heater hoses and install the alternator and warning switch cables.

Connect the vacuum hose, the throttle and choke wires and the air cleaner. Connect the starter motor cables and the fuel hose. Fit the coil, the distributor cap and the leads. Fit the radiator and re-make all hose connections.

Fill with coolant and engine oil and reconnect the battery. Fit the gear lever.

1.1.3. INSTALLATION — B20 E AND F ENGINE

Follow the previous installation instructions and carry out the following additional operations:

Fit the fuel injection components as the final installation operations. Connect the plug contact and lead to the distributor.

Remove the protective caps from the injectors and fit the injectors, distributor pipe and pressure regulator. Use new rubber seals on the injectors.

Fit the electrical contacts for the temperature sensor, cold start valve and throttle valve switch. Connect the hose for the pressure sensor and the induced air.

1.2. Engine — General Dismantling

Dismantling of the engine will be much easier if it can be mounted in the special swivel stand and attachment available under part numbers SVO 2520 and 2521. Block off all the manifold entries and give the exterior of the engine a preliminary clean to remove all loose dirt and oil.

Follow the order of removal of parts as given below. Further information on individual units can be found in the sections commencing at 1.4.

Remove the starter motor and take off the reinforcing plate under the flywheel housing. Remove the flywheel housing together with the gearbox and then remove the clutch and flywheel. Remove the flange from the rear of the engine, taking care not to damage the flange surfaces.

Remove the alternator, or dynamo, and then the water pump and distributor, the rocker cover and rocker arms and shaft and then the manifold. Take off the oil filter and then the cylinder head.

Lift out the push rods and keep them in their proper order. Remove the tappets from the cylinder block with tool SVO 2424 as shown in Fig. 2.

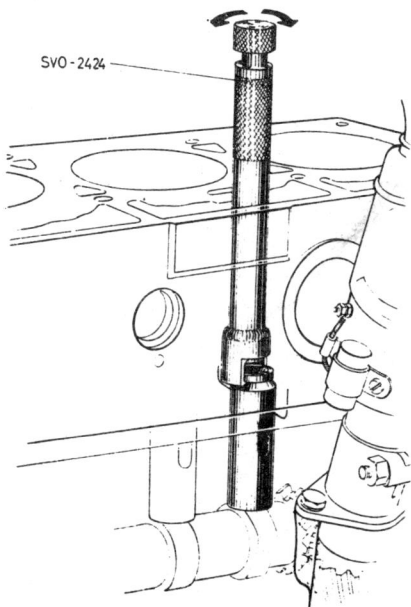

Fig. 2. — Removing the tappets with tool SVO 2424.

Remove the timing gear casing and the timing gears. Remove the camshaft. Remove the carbon ridge from the cylinder bores and invert the engine to remove the sump, oil pump and connecting rod caps. Push out the pistons and connecting rods and immediately replace the caps and bearings in their proper position on the rods. Keep all parts in their cylinder order.

Note that the main bearings are marked 1 to 5 from the front of the engine and the big end caps 1 to 4, again from the front.

Remove the main bearing caps and take out the crankshaft. Replace the caps in their proper position and keep the bearing shells together.

Clean all parts thoroughly, paying particular attention to the cylinder block oilways. All sealing plugs must be removed for proper cleaning to take place.

Do not wash aluminium parts in caustic soda. Use white spirit or fuel and dry with a blast of compressed air.

1.3.   Engine — Assembly

When assembling the engine, follow the general procedures outlined in this section and refer to the later sections for any detailed information that is necessary.

Lubricate all sliding or rotating surfaces with clean engine oil before assembling. Adhesive or sealer should not be used on the gaskets.

The seals on the ends of the oil pump delivery pipe and the water pump pipes are of special rubber and only genuine Volvo parts should be used. Fitting is facilitated by coating the rings with a soap solution.

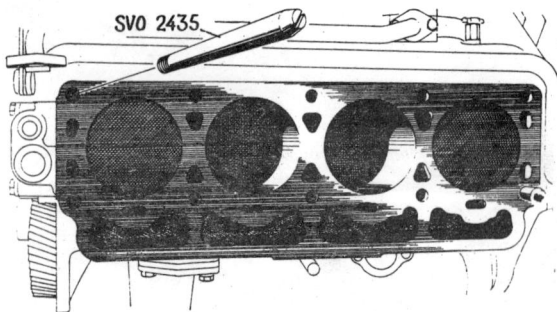

Fig. 3. — Fitting guide pins (SVO 2435) before placing the cylinder head in position.

The timing gear casing and the rear sealing flange must be accurately centred when refitting and details are given under the appropriate sections. Fit the cylinder head by using guide pins (2435) as shown in Fig. 3.

Install the new cylinder head gasket with the "Top" upwards. Install the water pump sealing rings and fit the head. Tighten the bolts in the order shown in Fig. 4 and in three stages (oil the threads first):

Stage 1: 4 kgm (29 lb.ft.)
Stage 2: 8 kgm (58 lb.ft.)
Stage 3: 9 kgm (65 lb.ft.) (after running the engine for 10 minutes)

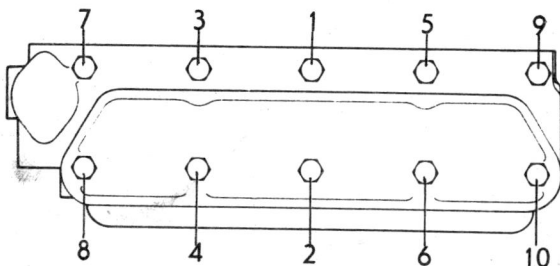

Fig. 4. — Tightening sequence for the cylinder head bolts.

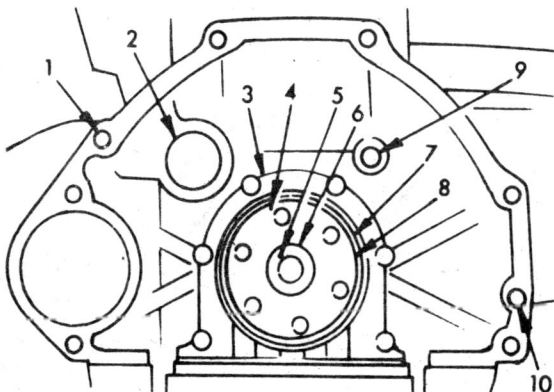

Fig. 5. — The rear end of the engine with the flywheel removed.

1.	Guide pin	6.	Circlips
2.	Core plug	7.	
3.	Sealing flange	8.	Sealing washer
4.	Crankshaft and pilot bearing	9.	Plug
5.		10.	Guide pin

17

Note that the initial valve clearance, for a cold engine, is set to:

For B20 A:	*0.45 - 0.50 mm*
	(0.018 - 0.020 in.)
For B20 B:	*0.55 - 0.60 mm*
	(0.022 - 0.024 in.)

For the B18 engines, use the cold valve clearances for initial setting. Lubricate the gearbox input shaft bearing in the flywheel with high-melting point grease.

Make sure that the cylinder head gasket is the correct one for the engine. Tighten all bolts and nuts to the torque settings given.

1.4. Engine — Servicing and Overhaul

1.4.0. CYLINDER HEAD AND VALVES

1.4.0.0. Technical Data

Head Height; Joint Face to
Face for Bolt Head:

B18:	*88.0 mm (3.46 in.)*
B20 A:	*86.7 mm (3.41 in.)*
B20 B:	*86.2 mm (3.39 in.)*
B20 E:	*84.9 mm (3.34 in.)*
B20 F:	*87.0 mm (3.42 in.)*

Gasket Thickness, uncompressed:

B20 A:	*1.4 mm (0.055 in.)*
B20 B and E:	*0.8 mm (0.031 in.)*
B20 F:	*1.2 mm (0.047 in.)*

VALVES

Valve seat angle:	*44.5°*
Seat angle in head:	*45°*

Seat Width in Head:

B18:	*1.4 mm (0.055 in.)*
B20:	*2.0 mm (0.080 in.)*

Valve Clearance:

B18 - Hot:	*0.40 - 0.45 mm*
	(0.016 - 0.018 in.)
- Cold:	*0.50 - 0.55 mm*
	(0.020 - 0.022 in.)
B20 A, E and F, Hot/cold:	*0.40 - 0.45 mm*
	(0.016 - 0.018 in.)
B20 B, Hot/cold:	*0.50 - 0.55 mm*
	(0.020 - 0.022 in.)

Valve Head Diameter:

Inlet — B18:	40 mm (1.58 in.)
— B20:	44 mm (1.732 in.)
Exhaust:	35 mm (1.378 in.)

Stem Diameter:

Inlet — B18:	8.685 - 8.70 mm (0.3419 - 0.3425 in.)
— B20:	7.955 - 7.970 mm (0.3132 - 0.3138 in.)
Exhaust — B18:	8.645 - 8.660 mm (0.3403 - 0.3409 in.)
— B20:	7.925 - 7.940 mm (0.312 - 0.3126 in.)

VALVE GUIDES

Length:

B18 — Inlet and exhaust:	63 mm (2.48 in.)
B20 — Inlet:	52 mm (2.047 in.)
— Exhaust:	59 mm (2.323 in.)

Bore Diameter:

B18:	8.725 - 8.740 mm (0.3435 - 0.3441 in.)
B20:	8.00 - 8.022 mm (0.320 - 0.321 in.)

Height above Cylinder Head Face:

B18:	21.0 mm (0.83 in.)
B20 A and B:	17.5 mm (0.689 in.)
B20 E and F:	17.9 mm (0.705 in.)

Clearance, Stem to Guide:

B18 — Inlet:	0.025 - 0.055 mm (0.001 - 0.0022 in.)
— Exhaust:	0.065 - 0.095 mm (0.0026 - 0.0037 in.)
B20 — Inlet:	0.030 - 0.068 mm (0.0012 - 0.0026 in.)
— Exhaust:	0.060 - 0.097 mm (0.0024 - 0.0038 in.)

VALVE SPRINGS

Free length:	46 mm (1.81 in.)
Load at 40 mm (1.57 in.):	29.5 ± 2.3 kg (65 ± 5 lb.)
Load at 30 mm (1.18 in.):	82.5 ± 4.3 kg (181.5 ± 9.5 lb.)

WEAR LIMITS

Max. clearance valve stems to guides:	0.15 mm (0.006 in.)
Max. wear, valve stems:	0.02 mm (0.0008 in.)

1.4.0.1. Servicing

The valve, guide and spring are shown in Fig. 6. Remove the valves from the cylinder head by using a spring compressor and removing the two halves of the collets.

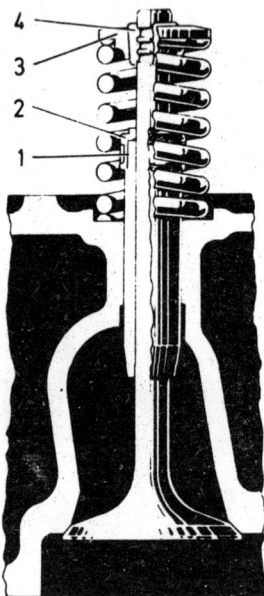

Fig. 6. — Valve, guide and valve parts.

1. 2.	Metal ring and rubber seal
3.	Washer
4.	Valve collet

Place the valves in a suitable rack in their proper order. A good way to keep them in order is to obtain a sheet of corrugated cardboard and to punch each valve stem through the card in their order of removal. Do not forget to mark "Front" on the cardboard.

Measure the clearance of the stem in the guide. Set up a dial indicator to the valve stem and move the valve stem "across" the head (this is important since most wear occurs in this plane) and check the clearance. With a new valve the clearance should not exceed 0.15 mm (0.006 in.).

Check the valve to the specifications given in the preceding section. Remove all carbon and deposits from the valves, combustion chambers and ports.

Grind and lap the valves as necessary. Check the valve seats to the dimensions given. If the seat width is too wide, use a 70° cutter or stone from the inside or a 20° from the outside.

Replace the valve guides, if necessary, as shown in Fig. 7, noting the following points:

— SVO 2818 and 2819 (as shown in the illustration) are for the B20 engines; for the B20 E and F engines use a 0.4 mm (0.016 in.) thick washer between the tool and the head to obtain the correct "A" dimension.

— For the B18 engines use tools SVO 1459 and 2289 and NOT those shown in the illustration.

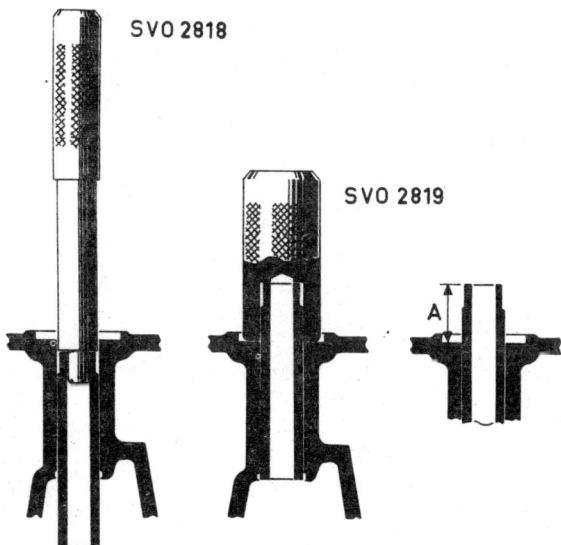

Fig. 7. — Removing and replacing the valve guides. The tools shown are for the B 20 engines.

If the wear between the rocker arm bush and the shaft amounts to 0.1 mm (0.004 in.) the bush should be replaced. Use tool SVO 1867 for removal and insertion and make sure that the oil hole in the bush lines up with the hole in the rocker arm. Ream the new bush to suit the shaft.

Grind the tip of the rocker arm only on a special machine. This is a job best entrusted to a dealer or distributor.

1.4.0.2. Adjusting the Valve Clearances

Valve clearances can be set with the engine either hot or cold, the values being given in the "Technical Data". Of the two values given for the different engines, the smaller should be regarded as a "Go" gauge and the larger as a "No-Go" gauge.

Adjust the valves in the following manner:

Place the No. 1 cylinder (nearest the front) at T.D.C. on its compression stroke (both valves closed) and adjust valves No. 1, 2, 3 and 5 (counting from the front). With the No. 4 cylinder at T.D.C. adjust valves 4, 6, 7 and 8.

1.4.1. PISTONS AND CONNECTING RODS

1.4.1.0. Technical Data

Pistons:	*Aluminium alloy*
Piston pin:	*Fully floating, with circlips*
Piston rings:	*2 compression (upper chromed), 1 oil control*
Connecting rods:	*Drop forged steel. Bushed at small end; shell bearing big ends.*
Max. deviation between pistons:	*10 g (0.35 oz.)*

PISTONS

Overall Length:	
B18 — Early models:	*83.5 mm (3.29 in.)*
— Later models:	*71 mm (2.79 in.)*
B20:	*71 mm (2.79 in.)*
Piston Running Clearance:	
B18:	*0.02 - 0.04 mm (0.0008 - 0.0016 in.)*

B20 A and B:	0.03 - 0.05 mm
	(0.0012 - 0.002 in.)
B20 E and F:	0.04 - 0.06 mm
	(0.0016 - 0.0024 in.)

PISTON RINGS

Width:
Compression rings:	1.98 mm (0.078 in.)
Oil control ring:	4.74 mm (0.186 in.)

Side Clearance to Groove:
B18 — Compression:	0.054 - 0.081 mm
	(0.0021 - 0.0032 in.)
B20 — Compression:	0.040 - 0.072 mm
	(0.0016 - 0.0028 in.)
Oil control:	0.040 - 0.072 mm
	(0.0016 - 0.0028 in.)

Ring Gap (in Cylinder):
B18:	0.25 - 0.50 mm
	(0.01 - 0.02 in.)
B20:	0.40 - 0.55 mm
	(0.016 - 0.022 in.)

PISTON PINS

Fit in connecting rod/piston:	Close running fit/push fit
Standard diameter:	22 mm (0.866 in.)

CONNECTING RODS

End float on crankshaft:	0.15 - 0.35 mm
	(0.006 - 0.014 in.)
Max. weight deviation:	6 g (0.21 oz.) in the set

Big End Bearing Shell U/S:
For B20:	0.010 and 0.020 in.
For B18:	0.010 in., 0.020 in., 0.030 in.,
	0.040 in. and 0.050 in.

1.4.1.1. Servicing

Measurement of the piston diameter must always be made at right angles to the piston pin bore. The measuring points are:

For B18 Engines:
Early models:	12.5 mm (0.49 in.)
Later models:	2.5 mm (0.098 in.)
For B20 engines:	12 mm (0.47 in.)

For the B18 engines, the measurement is made at the lower edge of the piston skirt with the micrometer anvils at the stated distance from the end. For the B20 engines, the position is similar but can be identified by the mark "71/14" on the crown face.

To check the fit of the piston in the cylinder bore, invert the piston (without the rings) and insert it into the bore with a feeler strip and a spring balance as shown in Fig. 8. For the B20 A and B engines, use a feeler strip of 1/2 in. width and 0.04 mm (0.0016 in.) thickness.

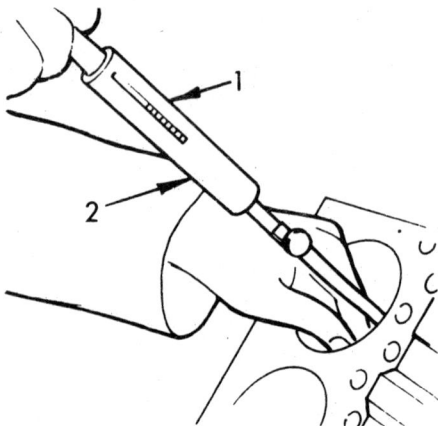

Fig. 8. — Checking the piston to cylinder clearance with a spring balance and feeler strip (refer to Section 1.4.2.2.).

For the B20 E and F engines use the same 1/2 in. width but have the thickness 0.05 mm (0.002 in.). For the B18 engines use a strip 0.03 mm (0.0012 in.) thick. If the clearance is correct then the force to withdraw the feeler strip should be 1 kg (2.2 lb.).

Check the piston ring gaps to the data given in Section 1.4.1.0. Push the ring down the bore, square it up by using an inverted piston and then measure the gap with a feeler gauge. Check the side clearance of the rings to their grooves as shown in Fig. 9.

Note that if the cylinder bore is worn that the ring gap measurement should be taken at the bottom dead centre position of the piston, where the wear is least.

Piston pins are available in three oversizes for the B18 engines (0.05 mm/0.002 in., 0.10 mm/0.004 in., 0.20

mm/0.008 in.), but only one size (0.05 mm/0.002 in.) for the B20 engines. If the piston pin hole is worn then ream out the bore so that the pin enters the hole with thumb pressure (use a piloted reamer).

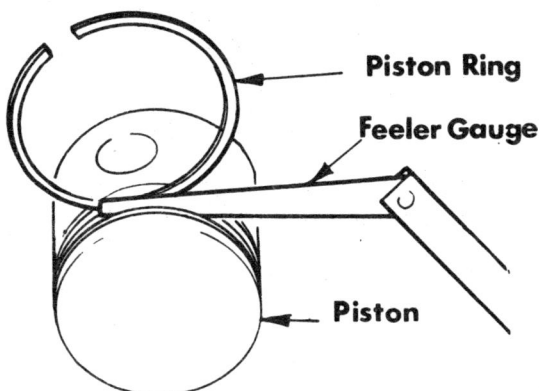

Fig. 9. — Measuring the ring-to-groove clearance.

Replacement of the small end bushes in the connecting rod is made with drift SVO 1867, or a made-up drift of the appropriate size. Make sure that the lubricating holes in bush and connecting rod are in alignment. Ream the bush to suit the pin so that it slides in under light thumb pressure. Check the connecting rods for bend or twist, using a proper alignment fixture.

Use a ring expander to fit the piston rings, noting that the top ring is the chromed one and that each ring is marked "Top".

Assemble the piston and connecting rod so that the arrow head (early models) or the slot (later models and B20 engines) is pointing forward, and the connecting rod marking is facing away from the camshaft side (see Fig. 10).

Lubricate the piston, rings and bearings and assemble into the cylinder, using a suitable ring compressor tool. Use new nuts and bolts for the big end bearing caps.

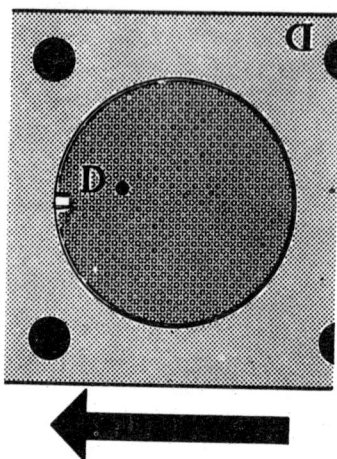

Fig. 10. — The marking on the piston crown. The arrow or the slot must face towards the front (arrowed).

1.4.2. CYLINDER BLOCK

1.4.2.0. Technical Data

Material:	*Alloy cast iron*

Cylinder Bores:
  Standard:
B20 A and B:	*88.91 mm (3.5004 in.)*
B20 E and F:	*88.92 mm (3.5008 in.)*

  Oversize (0.030 in.):
B20 A and B:	*89.67 mm (3.530 in.)*
B20 E and F:	*89.68 mm (3.531 in.)*
To be re-bored when wear amounts to:	*0.25 mm (0.010 in.)*

1.4.2.1. Servicing

Cylinder bores should be measured with a precision bore gauge and the measurement is to be made just below the head face and only in a transverse plane, across the engine axis. A letter is stamped on each cylinder bore to indicate the classification of the bore and the piston.

Particular care should be taken to thoroughly clean all cavities and passages and to remove all deposits and foreign matter.

1.4.3. CRANKSHAFT AND FLYWHEEL

1.4.3.0. Technical Data

Material:	*Forged steel, case-hardened*
Number of main bearings:	*5*
Thrust taken at:	*Rear flanged bearing*
Bearing type:	*Steel-backed shell type.*
	Lead/bronze, indium-plate
Main Bearing Journals:	
Standard diameter:	*63.451 - 63.464 mm*
	(2.4981 - 2.4986 in.)
Undersizes:	*0.010 and 0.020 in. (B20)*
Width on crankshaft for	
flanged bearing shell:	
Standard:	*38.960 - 39.00 mm*
	(1.5338 - 1.5351 in.)
Oversizes.	
No. 1 (0.010 in. U/S):	*39.061 - 39.101 mm*
No. 2 (0.020 in. U/S):	*39.163 - 39.203 mm*
Main bearings, radial	
clearance:	*0.028 - 0.083 mm*
	(0.0011 0.0033 in.) (B20)
Big End Bearing Journals:	
Width of bearing recess:	*31.950 - 32.05 mm*
	(1.2579 - 1.2618 in.)
Standard diameter:	*54.099 - 54.112 mm*
	(2.1299 - 2.1304 in.)
Undersizes:	*0.010 and 0.020 in.*
Big end bearings, radial	
clearance:	*0.029 - 0.071 mm*
	(0.0012 - 0.0028 in.)
B18 — Main Bearing, Radial	
Clearance:	
B18 A:	*0.026 - 0.077 mm*
	(0.0010 - 0.0030 in.)
B18 B:	*0.038 - 0.089 mm*
	(0.0015 - 0.0035 in.)

1.4.3.1. Servicing

Clean the crankshaft thoroughly and inspect for signs of scoring of the bearings and cracks. Measurement of the journals should be carried out at several points around the circumference and along the axis. Taper should not exceed 0.05 mm (0.002 in.) on any journal. Out-of-round for the main journals should not exceed 0.05 mm (0.002 in.) and 0.07 mm (0.003 in.) for the big end journals.

If the measurements are outside limits then the crankshaft should be ground undersize and suitable bearing shells fitted. Note that the B20 main and big end bearing shells are only available in undersizes of 0.010 and 0.020 in., but the B18 undersizes available are 0.01, 0.02, 0.03, 0.04 and 0.05 in.

Check the crankshaft straightness with a dial indicator to the centre bearing and the ends on "vee" blocks. The deflection of the dial indicator should not exceed 0.05 mm (0.002 in.). If it does, then the shaft will have to be straightened or replaced.

If re-grinding the crankshaft, note that the fillet radii (all journals) should be 2.0 - 2.5 mm (0.080 - 0.10 in.). The rear bearing journal will have to be ground to its proper width according to the undersize to be used.

Install the rear sealing flange with tool SVO 2439 as shown in Fig. 11. Make sure that the drain hole is not blocked by incorrect fitting of the sump gasket. Fit a new felt ring and also the washer and circlip.

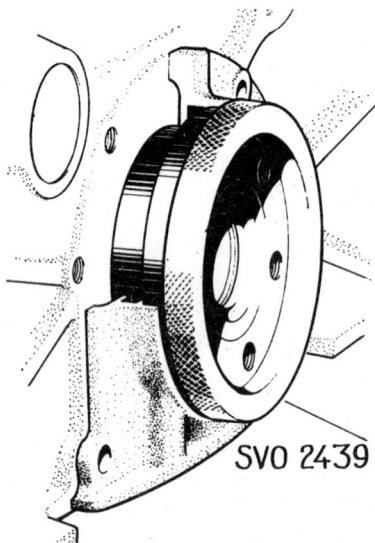

Fig. 11. — Centring the rear sealing flange with tool SVO 2439.

Flywheel: Check the run-out of the flywheel which must not exceed 0.05 mm (0.002 in.) at a diameter of

150 mm (5.9 in.). If the surface of the flywheel is scored or uneven it can be re-ground provided that no more than 0.75 mm (0.03 in.) is removed.

1.4.4. CAMSHAFT AND TIMING DRIVE

1.4.4.0. Technical Data

Camshaft:	*Alloy cast iron, case-hardened cams*
Timing drive:	*Single helical gears*
Number of camshaft bearings:	*3*
Valve operation:	*Tappets and push rods to rocker arms*
Camshaft Bearings:	
Radial clearance:	*0.02 - 0.075 mm (0.0008 - 0.003 in.)*
End float:	*0.02 - 0.06 mm (0.0008 - 0.0024 in.)*
Camshaft Marking/Lift Height:	
B18 A and B20 A:	*A/6.0 mm (0.24 in.)*
B18 B and B20 B:	*C/6.7 mm (0.26 in.)*
B20 E and F:	*D/7.2 mm (0.28 in.)*
Valve Clearance for Timing (cold Engine):	
B18 A and B20 A:	*1.10 mm (0.043 in.)*
B18 B and B20 B:	*1.45 mm (0.057 in.)*
B20 E and F:	*1.40 mm (0.055 in.)*
With above Settings, Inlet Valve should then open at:	
B18 A and B20 A:	*10° A.T.D.C.*
B18 B and B20 B:	*0° (T.D.C.)*
B20 E and B20 F:	*5.5° B.T.D.C.*
Timing Gear Backlash:	
Standard:	*0.04 - 0.08 mm (0.0016 - 0.0032 in.)*
Maximum:	*0.12 mm (0.0048 in.)*
Camshaft Wear Limits:	
Journal out-of-round, max:	*0.07 mm (0.0028 in.)*
Bearing wear, max:	*0.02 mm (0.0008 in.)*

1.4.4.1. Servicing

Note that the oil seal in the timing gear casing can be replaced without removal of the engine from the vehicle. The timing gears can also be replaced with the engine in the vehicle, but the radiator must be removed from the car to provide access.

To remove the timing gear casing, first remove the fan belt, fan and pulley and then the crankshaft pulley. Remove the timing gear casing, slackening and removing the front sump bolts as well. Remove the circlip and felt ring from the casing. Take off the hub from the crankshaft with tool SVO 2440 as shown in Fig. 12. Take off the crankshaft nut and check the backlash of the two gears before removal.

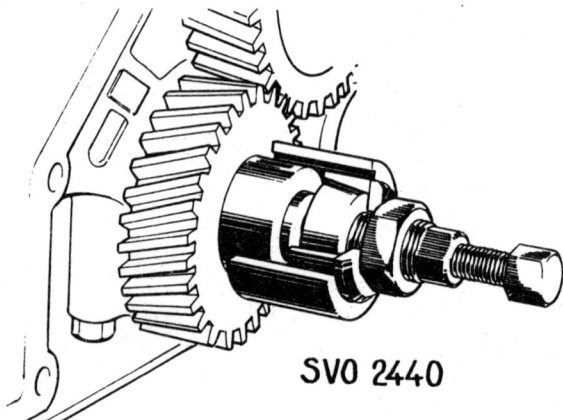

SVO 2440

Fig. 12. — Removing the crankshaft hub.

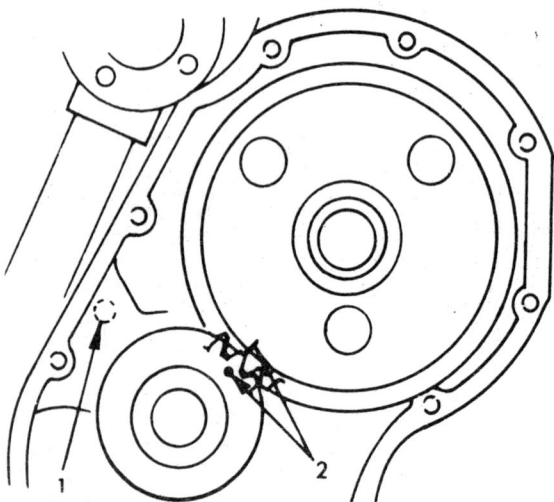

Fig. 13. — The timing marks (2) on the timing gears. Also note the nozzle for oil spray (1).

Pull off the crankshaft gear with tool SVO 2405 and then the camshaft gear with tool 2250. If these tools are not available then a simple extraction tool should be made up to engage with the tapped holes in the crankshaft gear or the holes behind the camshaft gear.

Refit the timing gears so that the marks are in line as shown in Fig. 13. Replace the crankshaft gear with tool 2408. Before replacing the camshaft gear, check that the axial clearance (end float) of the camshaft is within limits.

Before refitting the timing gear casing, check that the drain hole is clear. Install the casing and fit the bolts loosely. Centre the casing with tool SVO 2438 as shown in Fig. 14. The sleeve should be free as it is rotated.

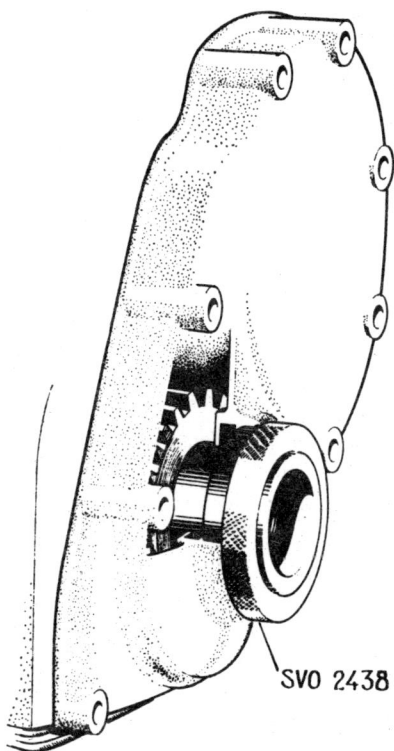

SVO 2438

Fig. 14. — Centring the timing gear casing before tightening the securing bolts.

Check this point again after the bolts have been tightened. Fit a new felt ring and then the circlip.

1.5. Engine — Tightening Torque Values

Cylinder head (oiled threads):	9.0 kgm (65 lb.ft.) (see Section 1.3.)
Main bearing caps:	12 - 13 kgm (87 - 94 lb.ft.)
Big end bearing caps:	5.2 - 5.8 kgm (38 - 42 lb.ft.)
Flywheel bolts:	5.0 - 5.5 kgm (36 - 40 lb.ft.)
Spark plugs:	3.5 - 4.0 kgm (25 - 29 lb.ft.)
Camshaft nut:	13 - 15 kgm (94 - 108 lb.ft.)
Crank pulley bolt:	7.0 - 8.0 kgm (50 - 58 lb.ft.)
Alternator bolt:	7.0 - 8.0 kgm (50 - 58 lb.ft.)
Nipple for oil filter:	4.5 - 5.5 kgm (32 - 40 lb.ft.)
Sump bolts:	8.0 - 11 kgm (60 - 80 lb.ft.)

1.6. Ignition System

1.6.0. DISTRIBUTOR

1.6.0.0. Technical Data

Distributor Type:	
B18 A:	Bosch JFR 4
B18 B, B20 A and B:	Bosch JFUR 4
B20 E:	Bosch JFURX 4
B20 F:	Bosch JFUX 4
Rotation:	Anti-clockwise
Breaker point gap (B20 B, E and F):	0.35 mm (0.014 in.)
Breaker point gap (B20 A):	0.35 mm (0.014 in.) min.
Breaker point gap (B18):	0.4 - 0.5 mm (0.016 - 0.02 in.)
Dwell angle:	59 - 65°
Contact pressure:	1.10 - 1.40 lb.
Firing order:	1 - 3 - 4 - 2
Ignition Timing (Vacuum Unit disconnected):	
B18 A (1,500 engine rpm):	21 - 23° B.T.D.C. (17 - 19° early models)
B18 B (1,500 engine rpm):	17 - 19° B.T.D.C.
B20 A (600 - 800 engine rpm):	14° B.T.D.C. (97 octane)
B20 B (600 - 800 engine rpm):	10° B.T.D.C. (100 octane)
B20 E (600 - 800 engine rpm):	10° B.T.D.C. (97 octane)
B20 F (600 - 800 engine rpm):	10° B.T.D.C. (94 octane)
Condensor capacity:	0.23 - 0.32 mfd

Distributor Centrifugal Advance begins at:	
B20 A:	600 - 1,000 rpm (E)
B20 B:	1,000 - 1,200 rpm (E)
B20 E:	750 - 1,100 rpm (E)
B20 F:	840 - 1,060 rpm (E)
Shaft axial play:	0.10 - 0.25 mm (0.004 - 0.01 in.)
Shaft to bush play, max.:	0.2 mm (0.008 in.)

1.6.0.1. Removal and Installation

Remove the distributor cap and take off the primary connection. Pull out the triggering contacts (B20 E and F only).

Remove the vacuum hose connection. Remove the clamp screw for the distributor body and lift out the unit. Before doing so, fit the rotor arm and mark its position in relation to the distributor body.

Install the distributor in the reverse sequence, making sure that the slot and groove mate together. If the engine oil pump has been removed or the engine has been rotated, the setting of the slot position must be carried out as described in Section 1.7.2.1.

1.6.0.2. Ignition Setting

The ignition timing should always be carried out with the engine running and with a stroboscopic timing lamp.

Clean the pulley so that the graduations can be seen. Disconnect the vacuum regulator and, if appropriate, take the following action:

— On the B20 B, pinch the hose with a clip to prevent the engine taking in unwanted air.

— On the B20 F with exhaust gas recirculation, the EGR valve should be disconnected.

Connect the timing light to the No. 1 cylinder and start the engine, checking that the speed is as given in Section 1.6.0.0. Slacken the distributor and turn it until the firing position agrees with the specification value.

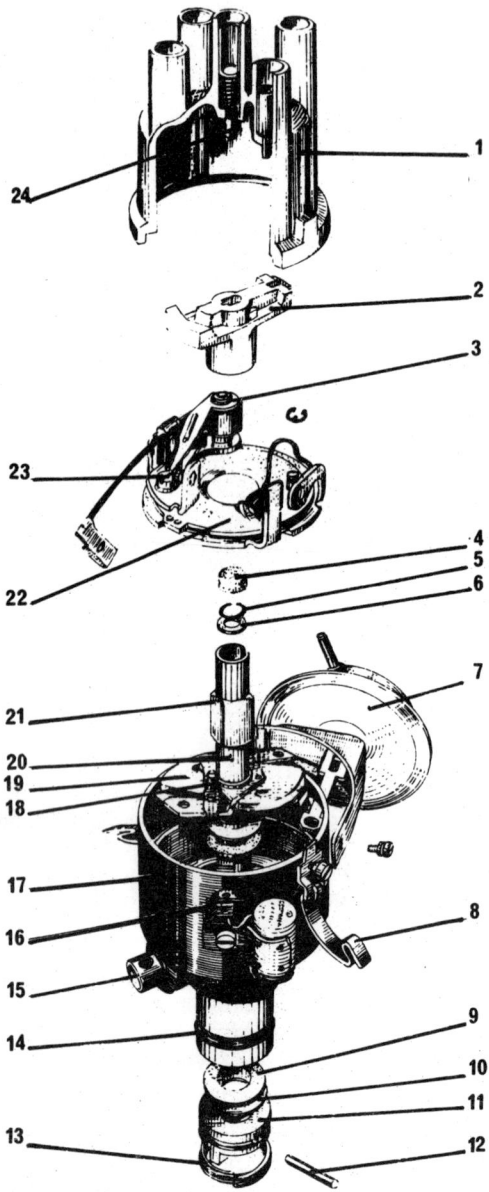

Fig. 15. — Typical distributor (B 20 B engine).

1.	Distributor cap
2.	and arm
3.	Contact breaker
4.	Lubrication felt
5.	Circlip and washer
6.	
7.	Vacuum regulator
8.	Cap clip
9.	Fibre washer and
10.	steel washer
11.	Driving collar and
12.	lock pin
13.	Soft ring
14.	Rubber seal
15.	Lubricator
16.	LT connection
17.	Distributor housing
18.	Centrifugal
	governor spring
19.	Weight
20.	Breaker cam unit
21.	Breaker cam
22.	Breaker plate
23.	Lock screw, breaker
	contacts
24.	Carbon contact

1.6.0.3. Setting and Replacing the Contact Breaker

The contact breaker can be replaced with the distributor fitted, but it is preferable to do so when the unit is dismantled.

Remove the rotor arm and disconnect the primary lead.

Remove the screw for the breaker and lift up the old contacts. Fit the new breaker, making sure that the unit is located correctly.

To adjust the gap, the fixed contact must be bent to obtain the correct gap (see "Technical Data"). This operation is best carried out with Bosch tool number EFAW 57 A. Make sure that the fibre block is resting on the highest point of the cam when adjusting the gap.

1.6.0.4. Maintenance

Lubricate every 10,000 km (6,000 miles). Place a few drops of oil into the cam screw head. Lightly grease the cam and the fibre tip. Apply one or two drops of oil to the advance mechanism.

Keep the breaker points free from grease or oil and wipe over the contacts with trichlorethylene.

1.6.0.5. Servicing

Typical distributors are shown in Figs. 15 and 16. Dismantling and servicing should be in accordance with the following notes:

Replace oxidised or burnt contacts. The colour of the contacts should be grey and the surfaces should be flat and smooth if they are to continue in service.

The radial play in the shaft and bushes should not exceed 0.2 mm (0.008 in.). If the bushes are replaced, do not forget that they are porous and must be soaked in light oil for an hour or so.

The play between the distributor shaft and the breaker cam must not exceed 0.1 mm (0.004 in.).

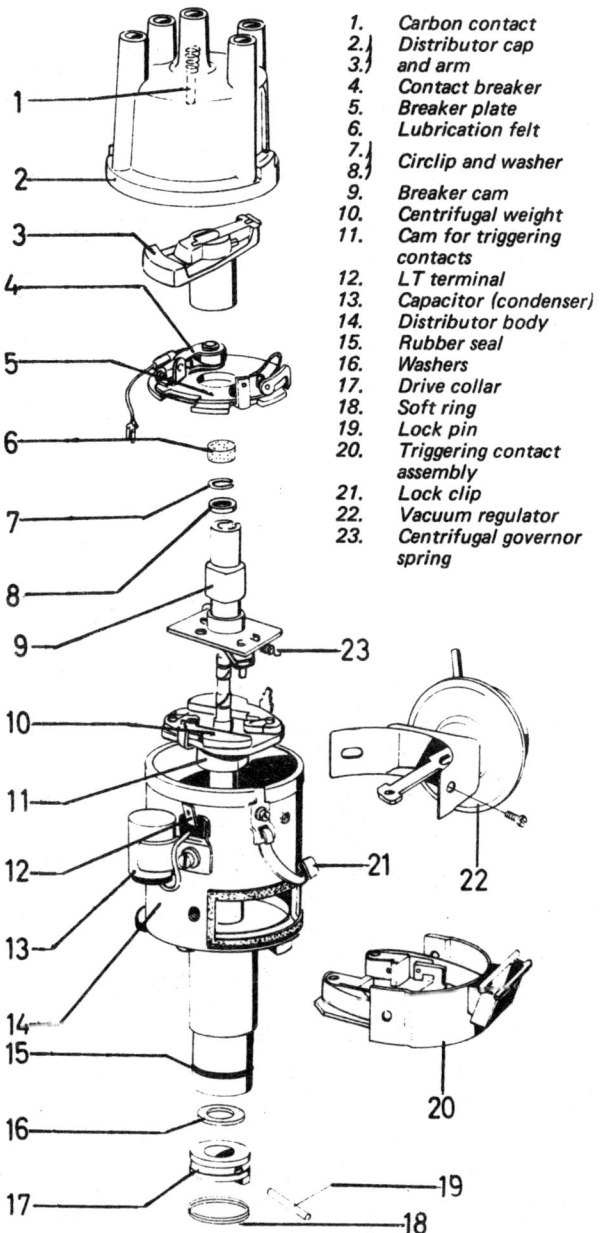

1. Carbon contact
2. Distributor cap
3. and arm
4. Contact breaker
5. Breaker plate
6. Lubrication felt
7.
8. Circlip and washer
9. Breaker cam
10. Centrifugal weight
11. Cam for triggering contacts
12. LT terminal
13. Capacitor (condenser)
14. Distributor body
15. Rubber seal
16. Washers
17. Drive collar
18. Soft ring
19. Lock pin
20. Triggering contact assembly
21. Lock clip
22. Vacuum regulator
23. Centrifugal governor spring

Fig. 16 — Distributor (fuel injection, 320 E and F).

The axial clearance of the shaft should be between 0.1 - 0.25 mm (0.004 - 0.01 in.). Any adjustment necessary can be made by altering the shaft adjusting washer thickness.

Mark the position of the breaker cam in relation to the shaft before dismantling.

Soak the lubrication felt pads in oil before assembling. The triggering contacts for the fuel injection engines cannot be adjusted and must be replaced if faulty or worn.

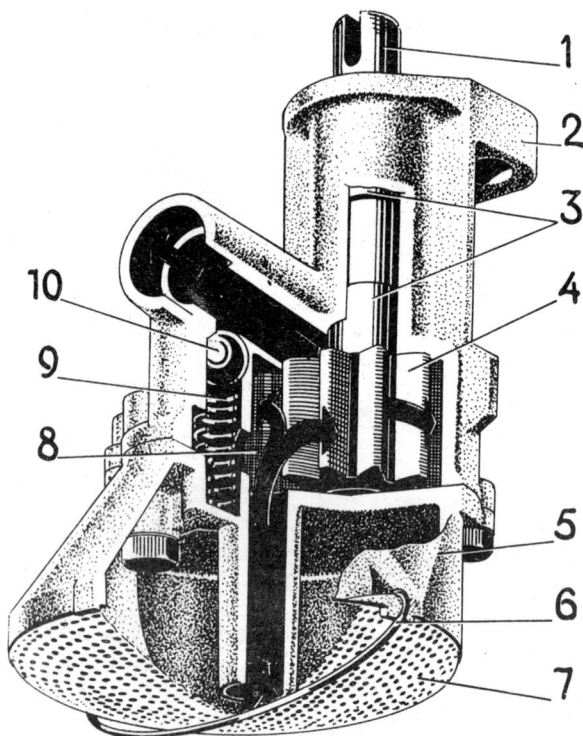

Fig. 17. — Part sectional view of the oil pump.

1.	Drive shaft	6.⎫	Retainer and strainer
2.	Pump body	7.⎭	
3.	Bushes	8.	Driven gear
4.	Drive gear	9.	Relief valve spring
5.	Cover	10.	Valve ball

It has not been possible, due to limitation of space, to include vacuum and centrifugal advance data for the various engines and distributors and we recommend that a dealer should be consulted if these features require checking. It is most important to ensure that the correct model of distributor is used for the vehicle being serviced.

1.6.1. IGNITION COIL

The ignition coil is mounted on the rear engine bulkhead (firewall). The unit cannot be dismantled but your dealer will have equipment to test the two windings. Keep the terminals and wiring clean and occasionally wipe over with a cloth moistened with fuel.

1.6.2. SPARK PLUGS

Thread:	*14 mm*
Electrode gap:	*0.7 - 0.8 mm*
	(0.028 - 0.032 in.)
Tightening torque:	*3.5 - 4.0 kgm (25 - 29 lb.ft.)*
Types:	
B18 A:	*Bosch W 175 T1*
B18 B:	*Bosch W 225 T1*
B20 A:	*Bosch W 175 T 35*
B20 B:	*Bosch W 200 T 35*
B20 E:	*Bosch W 240 T 35*
B20 F:	*Bosch W 200 T 35*
	or equivalent types

1.7. Lubrication System

1.7.0. TECHNICAL DATA

System Capacity:	
Including filter:	*3.75 litres (3.3 Imp. qt., 3.9 U.S. qt.)*
Excluding filter:	*3.25 litres (2.8 Imp. qt., 3.4 U.S. qt.)*
Engine Lubricant:	
Above −12⁰ C (+10⁰ F):	*SAE 20W/40 or 20W/50*
Below −12⁰ C (+10⁰ F):	*SAE 10W/30*
Oil pressure (hot engine at 2,000 rpm):	*2.5 - 6 kg/sq.cm (36 - 85 psi)*
Oil filter:	*Full flow, replaceable canister*

Oil Pump:	
Type:	Gear: 9 teeth each gear
End float:	0.20 - 0.10 mm
	(0.008 - 0.004 in.)
Radial clearance:	0.08 - 0.14 mm
	(0.0032 - 0.0055 in.)
Gear backlash:	0.15 - 0.35 mm
	(0.006 - 0.014 in.)
Relief valve spring:	
B18 — Free length:	32.5 mm (1.28 in.)
— Fitted length/load:	22.5 mm (0.89 in.)/
	8 kg (17.6 lb.)
B20 — Free length:	39 mm (1.54 in.)
— Load at 26.25	
mm (1.03 in.):	11 ± 0.88 lb.
— Load at 21 mm	
(0.83 in.):	15.4 ± 1.7 lb.

1.7.1. OIL COOLER

The B20 E engine (and the B20 F when fitted with exhaust emission control) is fitted with an oil cooler in which the engine coolant is used for heat transfer. The cooler is fitted between the oil filter and the cylinder block and the engine cooling system must be drained before the cooler is removed. Always use a new "O" ring to the connection to the cylinder block whenever the cooler is removed and replaced. Coat the "O" ring groove with Pliobond 20 before fitting the ring and tighten the securing nut to 3 - 3.5 kgm (23 - 25 lb.ft.).

1.7.2. OIL PUMP

1.7.2.0. Servicing

Note the installation of the oil pump as shown in Fig. 18; also note the special Volvo sealing rings as arrowed at the delivery pipe ends.

Clean the pump thoroughly after dismantling and inspect all parts for wear. Replace the shaft bushes if worn and ream them in position. Note that the shaft is only supplied with the gear and that it is recommended that both gears are replaced if wear is apparent.

Check the end float clearance, the radial clearance (gear teeth to body) and the gear backlash (see Fig. 19).

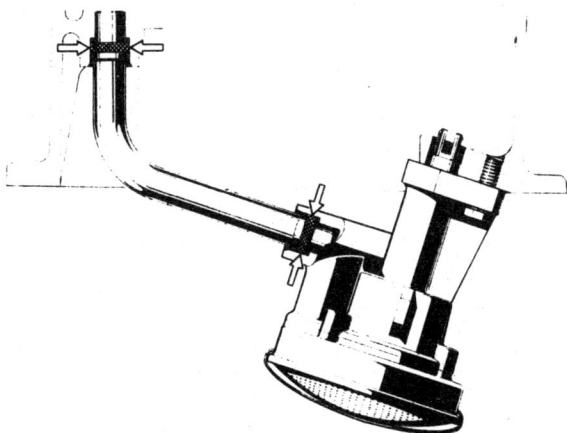

Fig. 18. — The oil pump in position, noting the two special seal rings (arrowed).

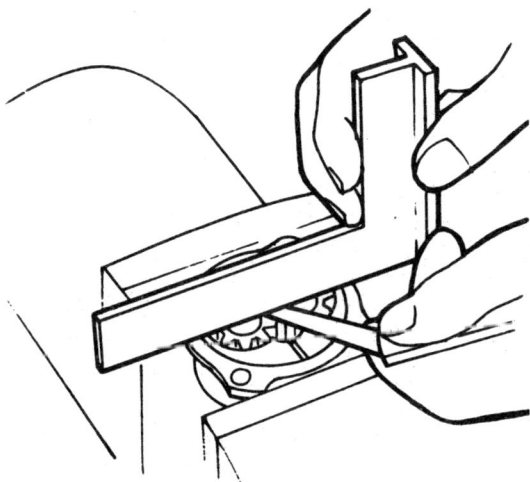

Fig. 19. — Measuring the end clearance between the gearwheels and the pump body face.

1.7.2.1. Installation of the Oil Pump

Install the oil pump and drive shaft with the No. 1 cylinder at T.D.C. on its firing stroke. In this position the slot should be as shown by "A" in Fig. 20 with the "A" value at approx. 35° for the B20 A engine and 5° for the B20 B, E and F engines.

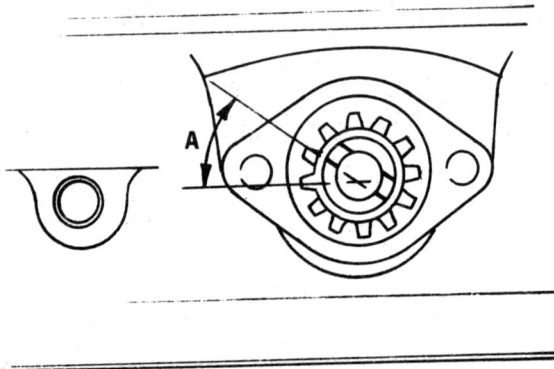

Fig. 20. – The installed position of the distributor drive shaft. The "A" angle for B20 A is 35° and for B20 B, E and F is 5°.

1.7.3. OIL FILTER

The oil filter should be replaced every 10,000 km (6,000 miles). The filter casing is unscrewed with a band-type tool and the complete canister discarded and replaced with a new part.

Smear the rubber gasket of the filter with oil before fitting and screw on the unit until the filter touches the cylinder block. Now screw in a further half turn by hand. Never use a tool for tightening.

1.8. Cooling System

1.8.0. TECHNICAL DATA

Type:	*Sealed system; thermo-syphon with impeller assistance*
Fan coupling:	*Conventional, fixed type; or fluid-slip type*

System (Cap) Pressure:
B18 engines:	0.23 - 0.3 kg/sq.cm (3 - 4 psi)
B20 engines:	0.7 kg/sq.cm (10 psi)

System Capacity:
B18 engines:	8.5 litres (2 Imp. gall., 2.25 U.S. gall.)
B20 engines:	10 litres (2.2 Imp. gall., 2.6 U.S. gall.)

Thermostat	Type 1 (Wax)	Type 2 (Wax)
Identification mark:	170	82°
Begins to open:	75 - 78° C (168 - 172° F)	81 - 83° C (177 - 181° F)
Fully open at:	89° C (192° F)	90° C (195° F)

Fan belt tension:	Refer to Section 12.3.

1.8.1.   WATER PUMP

To remove the water pump it is necessary to remove the
radiator in the case of the B20 engines. Slacken the
generator and remove the fan belt.

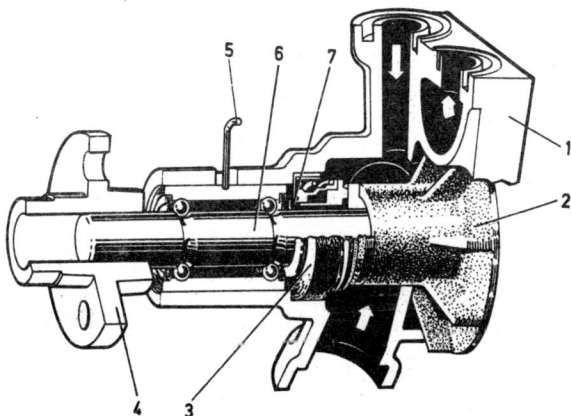

Fig. 21. — Section through the water pump.

1.	Housing	5.	Lock spring clip
2.	Impeller	6.	Shaft and bearings
3.	Seal ring		(cartridge unit)
4.	Flange	7.	Face seal

Remove the fan and pulley and then take out the water pump securing screws. The water pump is shown in Fig. 21 and it should be noted that the shaft and bearings form an integral unit that cannot be dismantled. If the pump is dismantled and the bearing cartridge is to continue in service then make sure that the unit is not washed in solvent since the lubricant will be contaminated.

To dismantle, press out the shaft from the pulley flange and remove the lock spring. Press out the bearing cartridge by pressing on the outer race. If the impeller is removed, as it must be to renew the seal, then it will be necessary to have a replacement since it is invariably damaged during removal.

Press on the impeller so that the flat side is flush to 0.4 mm (0.015 in.) below the housing face.

When refitting the pump, make sure that the mating surfaces are clean and that the seal rings are in position. Use a new gasket and press the pump upwards before tightening the bolts so that the seal rings make good contact.

1.8.2. RADIATOR

To remove the radiator, drain the cooling system by disconnecting the lower hose. Remove the expansion tank and drain the coolant. Remove the upper hose and remove the radiator bolts.

After refitting the radiator, fill with coolant through the filler opening with the heater control set to "Max.". Fill the expansion tank to the maximum mark and leave the expansion tank cap off while the engine is run for a few minutes. Top up as necessary and fit the expansion tank and main filler caps.

1.8.3. VISCOUS FAN COUPLING

Certain vehicles in the Volvo 140 series are fitted with a fan coupling which slips when the engine speed rises. The unit is not to be dismantled and must be replaced if faulty. When the water pump speed reaches about 3,500 rpm the fan should be rotating at about 2,250 rpm. As the engine speed increases still further, the fan coupling should reach its maximum of 2,500 rpm and then progressively reduce to about 2,000 rpm.

1.8.4. THERMOSTAT

The thermostat can be tested by suspending it in a container of water and gradually raising the temperature of the water. Suspend the thermostat with a piece of wire so that it does not touch the sides. The start of opening and the fully open values are given in Section 1.8.0. Discard a faulty thermostat. Always use a new gasket when refitting the housing.

1.8.5. FAN BELT TENSION

Refer to Section 12.3. for details of the fan belt tension. Note that there are different values for certain models.

Belt tension can be accurately checked with tool SVO 2906 if available. If the vehicle is fitted with an alternator, make sure that the rear end of the alternator is never subjected to any leverage or force. When fitting a new fan belt, final tensioning should be carried out after the belt has run for about 10 minutes.

1.9.   Fuel System — Carburettor Engines

1.9.0.   DESCRIPTION

The fuel system comprises a fuel tank, rear mounted, with a capacity of 58 litres (12.8 Imp. gall.) and a removeable filter located in the suction line.

Single or twin horizontal carburettors are used, either Zenith Stromberg or SU type. It is most important to remember that the carburettor fitted is dependent on the emission control features and, in some cases, the right-hand or left-hand drive of the vehicles. On no account can carburettors or parts be interchanged and spares and replacements should always be obtained by quoting the serial number and year of the vehicle in question.

Setting and balancing of twin carburettors is a skilled operation and requires special equipment to obtain the proper results. Vehicles with emission control features will only function properly if the ignition and fuel system are in good order and we suggest that your dealer or distributor should carry out such work with the special equipment they have for accurate setting and adjustment.

Vehicles fitted with fuel injection are dealt with separately in Section 13. Emission control is dealt with in Section 10. If the vehicle in question is fitted with any of these features, please read the sections mentioned before carrying out any work on the fuel system.

1.9.1. FUEL PUMP

1.9.1.0. Description

Two alternative types of fuel pump are used for the Volvo 140 series; one being manufactured by Pierburg and the other by S.E.V. The pump is a diaphragm type and a typical unit is shown in Fig. 22. For both types of pump the filter should be cleaned every 10,000 km (6,000 miles). A filter kit is available for each pump, but Volvo does not supply individual parts for the pumps currently in use. If the pump is defective it should be replaced.

1.9.1.1. Technical Data

Fuel Pump — Early Models:
  Type 1:   *Pierburg APG*
  Type 2:   *AC - YD*
  Fuel pressure:
    Minimum: *0.11 kg/sq.cm (1.5 psi)*
    Maximum: *0.25 kg/sq.cm (3.5 psi)*

Fuel Pump — Current Models:
  Type 1:   *Pierburg PE 15695*
  Type 2:   *S.E.V. 20005012*
  Fuel pressure:
    Minimum: *0.15 kg/sq.cm (2.1 psi)*
    Maximum: *0.28 kg/sq.cm (4.0 psi)*

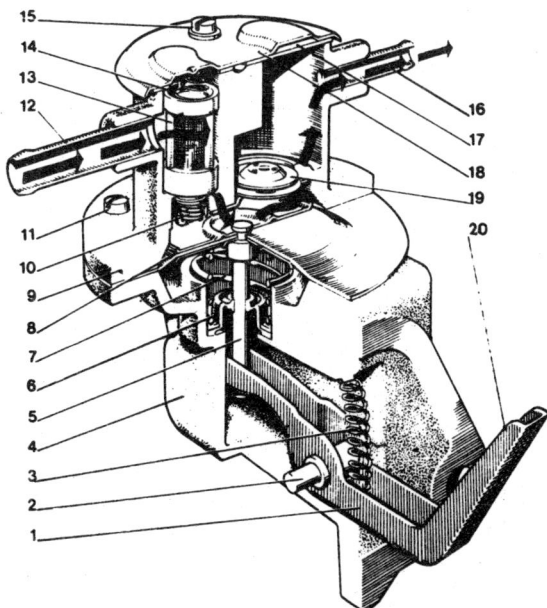

Fig. 22. — Section through a fuel pump (S.E.V.).

1. 2.	Rocker arm and shaft
3.	Spring
4.	Lower body
5.	Operating rod
6. 7.	Seal and spring
8.	Diaphragm
9.	Upper pump body
10.	Inlet valve
11.	Body screw
12.	Inlet
13. 14.	Filter and spring
15.	Cover screw
16.	Outlet
17. 18.	Seal and cover
19.	Outlet valve

1.9.2. AIR CLEANER

The air cleaner of the B18 B engine should be changed every 20,000 km (12,500 miles). All others at 40,000 km (25,000 miles). In severe driving conditions, with very dusty roads, change the filter more frequently.

47

Never attempt to clean the filters or wet them with any fluid. Do not run the engine with the air filter element removed.

1.9.3. CARBURETTORS

1.9.3.0. Introduction

It is most important to remember that the carburettor is an essential part of any exhaust emission control feature and that current practice is for the carburettor to be specially set by the manufacturer with the use of a CO-meter. It is not recommended that any adjustment or repair of such units be attempted by the owner. The general information given in the following sections should be carefully related to the actual carburettor being serviced and it must be noted that there are differences between some early and later versions of the same type of carburettor.

1.9.3.1. Technical Data

Carburettor Identification:

1967-69 ranges: 144S, 144, P142, P144 and 145:	*SU type HS6 or Zenith Stromberg 175 CD*
1970: 140 (B20 A):	*Zenith Stromberg 175 CD-2SE*
1970 : 140 (B20 B):	*2 x SU HS6 or 2 x Zenith Stromberg 175 CD-2SE*
B20 A:	*1 x Zenith Stromberg 175 CD-2SE*
B20 B (RHD):	*2 x Zenith Stromberg 175 CD-2SE*
B20 B:	*2 x SU, type HIF6*
B20 E and F:	*Fuel injection (see Section 13.)*

Idling Speeds:

1967-69, except as below:	*600 - 800 rpm*
1968-69: P152, 144 and 145 with B18 A:	*500 - 700 rpm*
Other models:	*800 rpm (700 rpm auto. transmission)*
Damping cylinder oil:	*Automatic transmission fluid type A*

Carburettors (Current Models):	*175 CD-2SE*	*SU-HIF6*
Air intake diameter:	*41.3 mm (1.63 in.)*	*41.3 mm (1.63 in.)*

48

Fuel Needle:		
B20 A:	B 1 CC	–
B20 B (RHD):	B 1 BL	–
B20 B:	–	BAZ
B20 B (Canadian market):	–	BBB

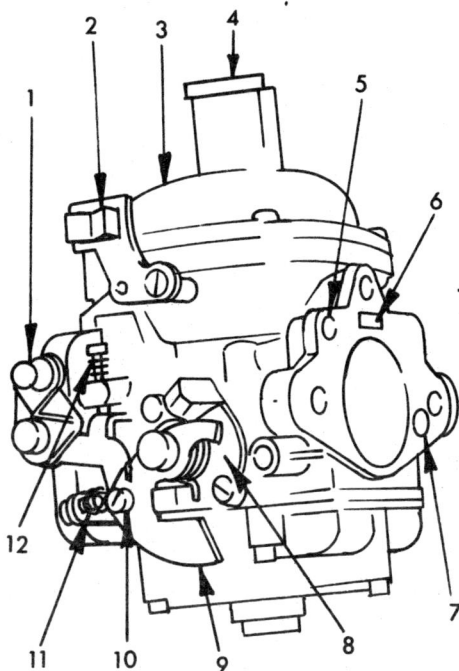

Fig. 23. – Zenith-Stromberg carburettor; left side (B20 A).

1. Lever for throttle control
2. Choke wire clamp
3. Suction chamber
4. Hydraulic damper
5. Float chamber vent drilling
6. Air supply dirlling
7. Drilling for air supply to temperature compensator
8. Cold start device
9. Cam disc, fast idle
10. Choke control connection
11. Fast idle stop screw
12. Throttle idle screw

1.9.3.2. Zenith-Stromberg Carburettor

Slow-Running and Fast Idle: Remove the air cleaner and press the air valve against the bridge. Screw in the adjusting screw until the jet touches the air valve. Unscrew the screw by 1 1/2 turns. Start the engine and run until it reaches operating temperature. Adjust the throttle stop screw until the engine idles at about 600 - 650 rpm. Now turn the screw downwards until the engine runs smoothly. Turn the screw in the opposite direction until the engine once again runs unevenly and set the final slow-running speed somewhere between the two screw positions.

Adjust the fast idle by turning the screw until the tip touches the fast idle cam at a point approx. 1/2 in. (11 - 13 mm) from the upper part, with the fast idle cam turned upwards.

Centralising the Jet: Screw up the orifice adjuster until the top of the orifice is just above the bridge. Slacken the jet assembly and place the carburettor so that the flange on the butterfly is facing downwards. Let the air valve fall down which will have the effect of centralising the jet. Slowly tighten the jet and check that the needle remains free. Check the centralisation by raising the valve with the lifter pin and make sure that a distinct "click" is heard as the valve strikes the bridge.

Float Level: Remove and invert the carburettor and remove the float chamber. With the needle resting on its seating the dimension "B" shown in Fig. 24 should be 15 - 17 mm (0.625 in.). For the early carburettors, the dimension "A" should be 4 - 8 mm (0.25 in.), while for the CD-2SE models it should be 9 - 13 mm (0.50 in.). Adjust by carefully bending the tab at the float valve.

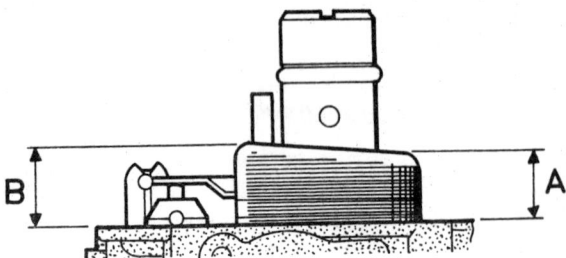

Fig. 24. — Float level adjustment (Stromberg).

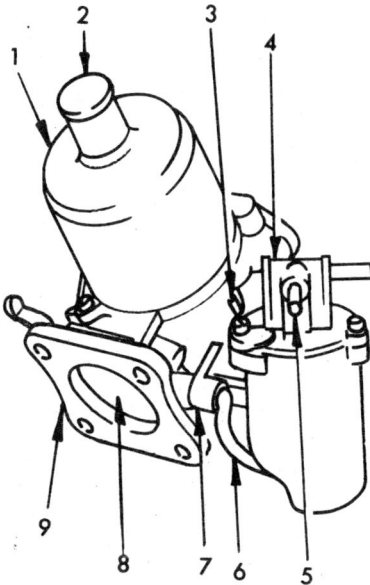

Fig. 25. — SU HS6 carburettor (left side).

1. Suction chamber
2. Damper piston screw
3. Lift pin
4. Float chamber cover
5. Ventilation hole
6. Fuel line
7. Lever
8. Throttle flap
9. Flange

1.9.3.3. SU Type Carburettors

Float Level: For B18 engines refer to Fig. 27. The distance from the rivet head of the float arm to the ridge of the float chamber is to be 3.2 mm (0.126 in.) for early models and 4.8 mm (0.189 in.) for later models. If the float level is incorrect, do not bend the float arm but replace the part. The setting is not critical since the carburettor is relatively insensitive to float level vari-

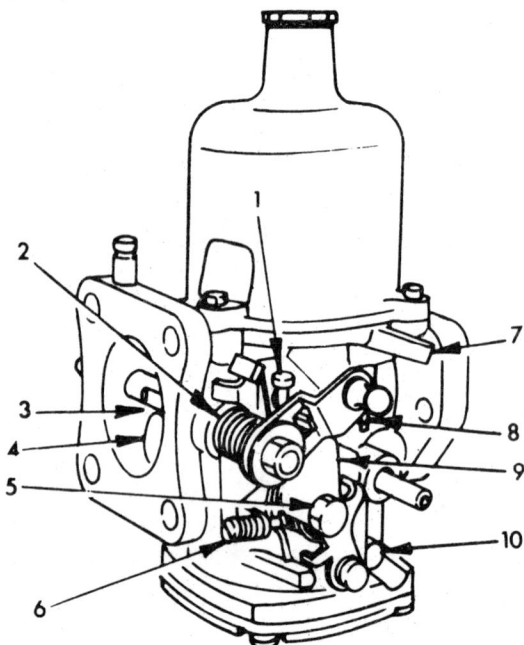

Fig. 26. — View of the SU HIF type carburettor.

1.	Stop	6.	Adjusting screw
2.	Return spring	7.	Carburettor housing
3.	Throttle valve	8.	Throttle lever
4.	Overrev valve	9.	Operating lever
5.	Cold start device	10.	Valve

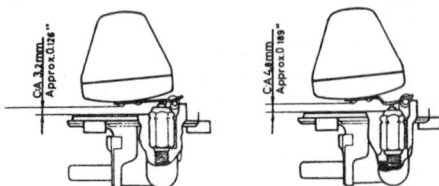

Fig. 27. — Checking the float level on SU HS6. Early models on the left, later models on the right.

ations. For the B20 engines, refer to Fig. 28 and set the "A" dimension to 0.5 - 1.5 mm (0.02 - 0.06 in.) by bending the metal tab.

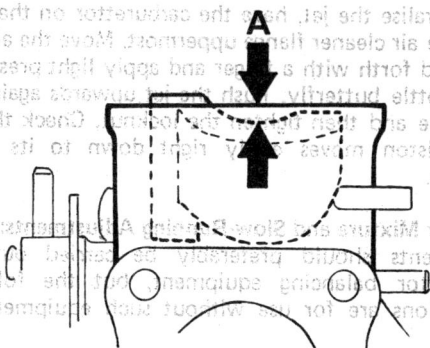

Fig. 28. — Float level adjustment on the SU HIF carburettor.

Centralising the Jet: Fit the metering needle so that the face of the cylindrical portion is flush with the end of the piston. For the SU HIF type carburettors (B20), refer to Fig. 29 and note the spring under the needle.

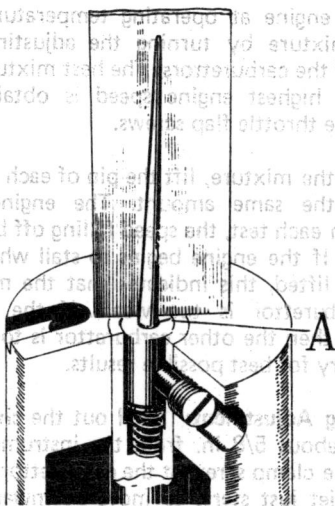

Fig. 29. — Fitting the metering needle on the SU HIF carburettor.

The needle should incline in the direction of the air cleaner flange and this will be obtained when the line "A" is in the position shown.

To centralise the jet, have the carburettor on the bench with the air cleaner flange uppermost. Move the air valve back and forth with a finger and apply light pressure to the throttle butterfly. Push the jet upwards against the jet sleeve and then tighten the locknut. Check that the valve piston moves easily right down to its lowest position.

Fuel/Air Mixture and Slow-Running Adjustments: These adjustments should preferably be carried out with carburettor balancing equipment, but the following instructions are for use without such equipment (SU HS6):

Screw the adjusting nuts of both carburettors to their upper position and then back by 1 1/2 turns, make sure both are equal.

Adjust the throttle flap stop screws so that they just touch the levers when the flaps are closed, then tighten by half a turn.

With the engine at operating temperature, adjust the fuel/air mixture by turning the adjusting nut at the bottom of the carburettors. The best mixture is obtained when the highest engine speed is obtained, without altering the throttle flap screws.

To check the mixture, lift the pin of each carburettor in turn by the same amount. The engine should run equally on each test, the speed falling off by about 100 - 150 rpm. If the engine begins to stall when one of the pistons is lifted, this indicates that the mixture in the other carburettor is too weak. If the engine speed increases, then the other carburettor is too rich. Adjust as necessary for best possible results.

Fast Idling Adjustment: Pull out the choke operating cable by about 5/8 in. from the instrument panel and slacken the clamp screw at the carburettor. Lift the lever until the jet just starts to move downwards and adjust the fast idle cam to this position. Tighten the clamp screw at this position. Pull out the choke operating cable by about 13/16 in. (20 mm) and have an assistant check that both jets are moving downwards by the same amount.

1.9.3.4. Damper Piston (Carburettors)

Every 10,000 km (6,000 miles) check the level of oil in the damper cylinder. Always check this point before commencing any adjustment of the carburettors. If the engine does not react properly during acceleration, check the end float on the damper plunger. It is essential that there is an end play of 1.0 - 1.8 mm (0.04 - 0.07 in.) for correct operation.

For early models, the recommended fluid is light engine oil but for all current models the manufacturers recomment Automatic Transmission Fluid Type A.

2. CLUTCH

2.0. Description

The clutch for the 140 series vehicles is a single dry plate type with a diaphragm spring. The clutch is operated by a pendant pedal, with a flexible wire assembly transmitting the pedal movement to a release fork and a ball-type release bearing.

All models use the same size and specification of clutch but there are two versions with a difference in design of the clutch cover. The three major components of the clutch unit comprise a clutch plate, pressure plate and a clutch cover. The clutch disc assembly is fitted with rivetted-on facings and the facings can be replaced. The pressure plate and the cover assembly cannot be dismantled and must be replaced if faulty.

2.1. Technical Data

Type:	*Single dry plate, diaphragm spring*
Size:	*8.5 in.*
Clutch friction area (total):	*440 sq.cm (68.2 sq.in.)*

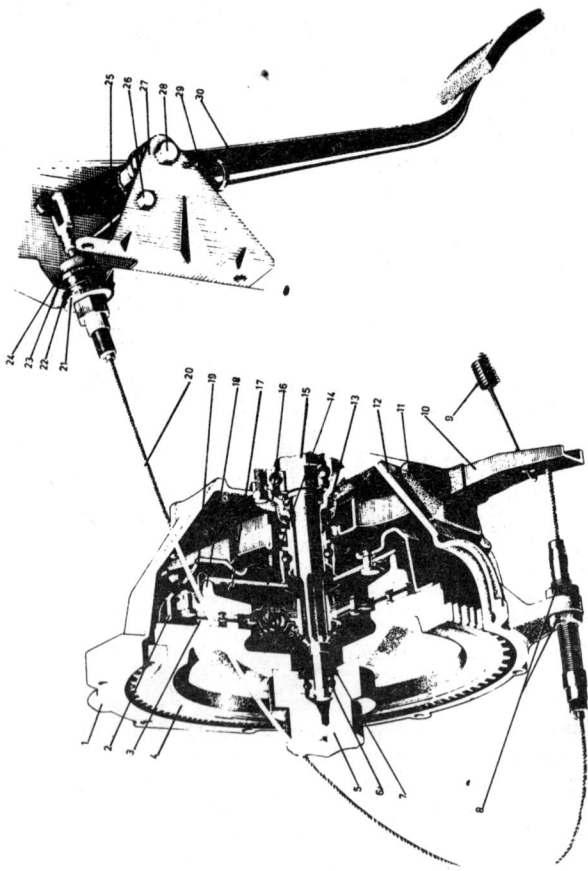

Fig. 30. — The clutch and clutch controls.

1. Flywheel cover
2. Clutch cover
3. Clutch plate
4.⎫
5.⎬ Flywheel and crankshaft
6. Input shaft bearing
   (pilot bearing)
7. Circlip
8.⎫
9.⎬ Adjusting nuts and
   return spring
10.⎫
11.⎬ Release fork and
   dust cover
12. Holding plate
13. Release bearing
14. Diaphragm spring
15. Input shaft (gearbox)

16. Cover (gearbox)
17. Support rings
18. Pressure plate
19. Retainer
20. Clutch cable
21.⎫
22.⎬ Washer and
   rubber bush
23.⎫
24.⎬ Washer and nut
25. Rubber sleeve
26. Bolt for pedal stop
27. Bracket
28. Bolt for pedal shaft
29.⎫
30.⎬ Return spring and
   clutch pedal

57

Clutch Pedal Travel:
   B20 — LHD: 150 mm (6.0 in.)
      — RHD: 160 mm (6.4 in.)
   B18 models: 125 - 130 mm
                            (4.9 - 5.12 in.)

Release fork travel: 3 mm (0.12 in.)
Clutch disc rivet diameter: 3.5 mm (0.14 in.)
Pressure plate flatness: Zero convex to 0.03 mm
                            (0.0012 in.) concave

2.2.   Replacing the Control Cable

The clutch control cable can be replaced without removing the clutch assembly from the vehicle by proceeding as follows:

Unhook the release fork return spring. Slacken the front and rear nuts and disconnect the wire from the release fork.

Loosen the cable clamp at the wheel reinforcing member and remove the panel under the dashboard. Take off the pedal bearing bolt and disconnect the wire from the pedal connection. Slacken the nut for the cable sleeve and remove the unit from the car.

Install in the reverse sequence to removal. Adjust the free play as described later.

2.3.   Servicing the Clutch Pedal Assembly

To replace the pedal or the pedal bushes refer to Fig. 31.

Unhook the return spring from the pedal and remove the bolt and nut. Disconnect the wire and remove the pedal assembly.

Take out the tubular shaft, inspect the bushes and drive them out if necessary. Fit new bushes and lubricate with MP grease.

Assemble in the reverse sequence and hook on the return spring.

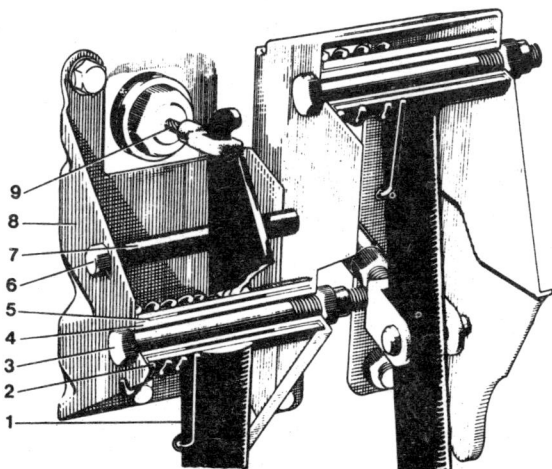

Fig. 31. — Clutch pedal assembly.

1.} Clutch pedal and
2.} return spring
3.} Bolt and shaft
4.}
5.   Bush
6.   Bolt, pedal stop
7.   Rubber sleeve
8.   Bracket
9.   Clutch cable

2.4.   Removal and Installation

To remove the clutch assembly, first refer to Section 3. and follow the instructions for removal of the gearbox.

Remove the upper bolt from the starter motor mounting. Take out the release bearing from the rear of the housing. Disconnect the cable from the release fork. Slacken the flywheel housing bolts and remove the housing.

Slacken the bolts from the clutch housing a little at a time, working in a diagonal pattern. Do this carefully to avoid distortion of the housing which is still under pressure from the clutch spring. Remove the release fork ball stud and the fork.

Install the clutch unit as detailed below. Before doing so carry out the servicing necessary and wash off flywheel, pressure plate and facings with petrol (gasoline) to remove all grease, oil and dirt.

Set up the clutch plate with the longest side of the hub backwards (towards the gearbox). Offer up the clutch assembly and centre the unit by inserting mandrel SVO 2484 into the pilot bearing.

Insert the six bolts into the flywheel and tighten gradually, a turn or two at a time, working in a diagonal pattern. Tighten fully and remove the mandrel.

Fit the release mechanism into the flywheel housing. Place the upper bolt for the starter motor into the housing and offer up the housing. Fit the bolts as follows:

(1)   The four upper bolts first, then the lower bolts for the starter motor.

(2)   The two lower (3/8 in.) bolts.

(3)   Fit the upper starter motor nut after the clutch cable has been fitted. Secure the wire end to the release fork and fit the release bearing. Fit and tighten the upper starter motor bolt nut.

Fit the gearbox as instructed in Section 3. and adjust the clutch pedal play.

2.5.   Servicing

2.5.0.   CLUTCH FACINGS

Replace the clutch facings if they show signs of burning or oil contamination or if the rivets are close to, or flush with, the lining surfaces. Drill out the old rivets with a drill of the same diameter as the rivets (see "Technical Data").

Check the clutch plate. It must not be warped, the springs and rivets must be secure and the plate must not be cracked. If any of these defects are found then the plate must be replaced.

Rivet on the new facings. Use every other hole and have the rivet heads on the facing side. Repeat for the other side facing. It is preferable to use a proper rivetting press for this operation.

Check that the spline drive is not worn or scored. Replace if necessary.

2.5.1.   CLUTCH ASSEMBLY

The clutch assembly cannot be dismantled and must be replaced if faulty. Check for heat damage, cracks, scoring or other faults to the pressure plate.

Place a straight edge or accurate ruler across the pressure plate and check the "bow" of the plate across its width.

The plate must not be convex (higher at the inner edge than the outer) but can be concave to the value given in the "Technical Data".

Check the diaphragm spring for cracking or damage and replace the complete unit if damage is found.

Inspect the release bearing under hand pressure. The bearing should turn smoothly without binding and should also slide easily on the guide sleeve.

2.5.2.   INPUT SHAFT (PILOT) BEARING

The flywheel input shaft bearing is removed, if necessary, with tool SVO 4090 and the new bearing pressed in with drift SVO 1426. Clean the bearing with petrol (gasoline) and re-pack with high-melting point grease. Do not apply excessive grease otherwise it may find its way onto the clutch facings.

2.6.   Clutch Pedal Free Play

Maintain or adjust the clutch pedal free play by adjusting the nuts of the cable sleeve (at the clutch housing) so that there is a free travel of 3 mm (0.12 in.) between the ball and the withdrawal lever. Lock the nuts securely when the adjustment is complete.

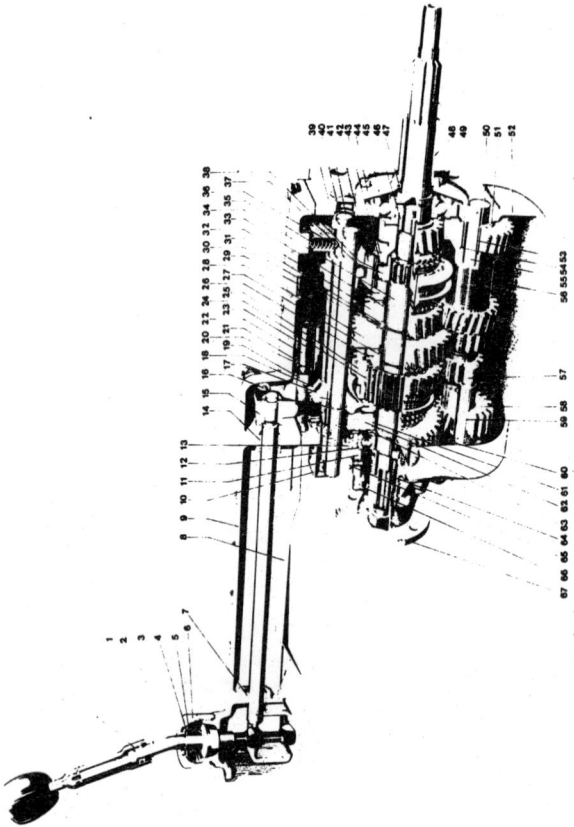

Fig. 32. – Section through the gearbox (M40) without overdrive.

1. Gear lever, upper and
2. lower sections with
3. rubber bushes
4. Washer and spring
5.
6. Cover
7. Bush
8. Bottom cover and
9. gearbox cover
10. End casing
11. Rear cover
12. Ball bearing
13. Striker (ghosted view)
14. Bush
15. Gearshift rod
16. Contact (reverse and belt reminder)
17. Selector fork, 1st/2nd

18. Gate
19. Sliding plate
20. Sleeve (reverse catch)
21. Spring and sleeve
22.
23. Spring
24. Insert
25. Engaging sleeve and gear, reverse
26. Synchroniser cone
27. Needle bearing bush
28. Synchroniser cone
29. Thrust washer
30. Circlip
31. Thrust washer
32. 3rd speed gear
33. Bush, needle bearing
34. Main shaft

35. Spring and
36. interlock ball
37. Synchroniser hub
38. Insert
39. Selector rail, 3rd/4th
40. Selector rail, 1st/2nd
41. Selector rail, reverse
42. Engaging sleeve
43. Spring
44. Synchroniser cone
45. Ball bearing
46. Roller bearing
47. Oil seal
48. Cover
49. Input shaft
50. Spacer washer
51. Thrust washer
52. Housing (main casing)

53. Needle bearing
54. Spacer washer
55. Countershaft (layshaft cluster)
56. Layshaft
57. Reverse shaft
58. Reverse gear
59. Bush
60. Striker lever (ghosted view)
61. Bush, needle bearing
62. 1st speed gear
63. Thrust washer
64. Speedometer drive gear
65. Vent nipple
66. Oil seal
67. Flange and nut

63

3.   TRANSMISSIONS

3.0.   Description

The Volvo 140 series vehicles may be fitted with a four-forward speed and reverse gearbox, a 4-speed gearbox with overdrive or a 3-speed automatic transmission.

The 4-speed manual gearbox has synchromesh on all forward speeds and is shown in Fig. 32 in the design adopted for all current vehicles. Earlier vehicles use a box of the same internal design but the gear lever is fitted directly to the top cover without the extension rod and extension housing of the current design. Note also that the 1973 range of vehicles has been modified on the first gear ratio as compared with earlier models.

Servicing and overhaul of the manual gearbox and overdrive is dealt with as for the current design vehicles, with the differences detailed in the "Technical Data", and in the text as necessary, for the earlier model.

The overdrive, when fitted, is attached to the rear of the standard gearbox with the facility that the unit can be removed from the gearbox as a complete assembly. The overdrive function is provided by hydraulic power, from a built-in pump and filter, and the operation is by electrical solenoid and switch.

The automatic transmission is a Borg-Warner three-element torque convertor followed by a hydraulically operated planetary gear train giving three forward gear ratios and reverse. The selector control is provided with the usual positions for "P", "R", "N", "D", "2" and "1".

Certain tools are required for servicing of the manual gearbox and we recommend that these should always be employed, or alternative equipment made up. The servicing of the overdrive is complicated, as must be expected with a hydraulically operated unit. It is not recommended that the owner should attempt such work unless he is familiar with the servicing of high precision hydraulic components and has available the necessary workshop conditions and tools.

Servicing of automatic transmissions is highly complicated and cannot be carried out without special tools and checking equipment. We do not recommend that the owner should attempt such work and we do not attempt to give more than a general outline of the unit with routine information.

3.1.   Manual Gearbox

3.1.0.   TECHNICAL DATA

Type designation:	*M 40*
Reduction Ratios:	
1st gear:	
1973 models:	*3.41 : 1*
Earlier models:	*3.13 : 1*
2nd gear:	*1.99 : 1*
3rd gear:	*1.36 : 1*
4th gear (top):	*1 : 1*
Reverse gear:	*3.25 : 1*
Lubricant:	*Gear oil: SAE 80. Alternative- ly Engine Oil SAE 30*
Lubricant capacity:	*0.75 litres (2.8 Imp. pints, 1.56 U.S. pints)*
Lubrication Service (change oil):	
New or re-conditioned box:	*After the first 5,000 km (3,000 miles)*
Thereafter:	*Every 40,000 km (25,000 miles)*

3.1.1.   REMOVAL AND INSTALLATION

Attach lifting tool SVO 2727 onto the engine, placing the lifting hook round the exhaust pipe. Take the weight on a hoist or crane.

Remove the gear lever. Jack up the vehicle and support on suitable stands at the front and rear. Drain the oil from the gearbox. Loosen and remove the supporting member from under the gearbox.

Disconnect the front universal joint from the gearbox flange. Disconnect the speedometer cable. Take off the rear engine mounting and the bracket for the exhaust pipe.

Lower the rear end of the engine by about 20 mm (0.8 in.) and disconnect the cable for the reversing (back-up) light and, if fitted, the overdrive cable. Slacken and remove the upper right and lower left gearbox bolts. Fig. 33 shows how this operation must be carried out with the special flexible joint tool (SVO 2427) and the other tools.

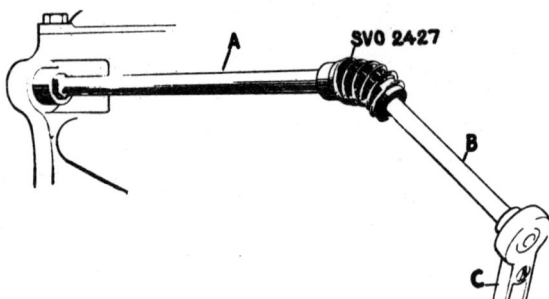

Fig. 33. — The special tools for removal and insertion of the gearbox bolts.

A.   SVO 2487
B.   Extension with 3/8 in. square
C.   Ratchet handle

Fit a guide pin (SVO 2743) into each of the holes where the bolt has been removed and then remove the remaining two bolts. Withdraw the gearbox from the guide pins and lower to the ground.

Installation of the gearbox (or the gearbox and overdrive) is carried out in the reverse sequence to removal.

Note that the two guide pins must be in position before the box is lifted back. DO NOT forget to replace with the bolts. Fill the gearbox with the recommended lubricant.

3.1.2. REPLACING THE GEARBOX REAR OIL SEAL

The rear oil seal can be replaced without removal of the gearbox by carrying out the following operations:

Follow the instructions in the previous section as far as lowering the engine.

Slacken the flange nut. To do this it will be necessary to hold the flange from rotation. Use the special pin-type wrenches available: SVO 2854 for vehicles with B20 A, B or F engines and SVO 2837 for the B20 E engine. Pull off the flange with a suitable puller or tool SVO 2261.

Remove the old oil seal with puller SVO 4030 and fit the new seal with sleeve SVO 2413.

Press on the flange with tool SVO 2304. Do not forget to lubricate the oil seal lip with a little oil before assembly. Complete the installation as in the previous section.

3.1.3. DISMANTLING

The description and instructions given in this section and the section on assembly apply only to the gearbox itself.

Instructions are given for the differences in dealing with the main shafts for both overdrive and non-overdrive type boxes but the overdrive itself should be removed from the main box and dealt with separately in accordance with the appropriate sections.

To dismantle the gearbox, mount it in a suitable fixture. SVO 2922 is the recommended fixture. SVO 2520 is the accompanying floor-mounted attachment for the fixture but is not essential.

Unscrew the bolts for the gearbox cover and lift it off. Carefully remove the springs and balls for the selector mechanism. Remove the cover over the selector rails and unscrew the screws securing the selector forks to the rails.

Slide the selector fork backwards to the 1st speed position and drive out the pin part-way (it must not foul the 1st speed gear). Now move the selector fork forwards to allow the pin to pass in front of the gear and then drive out the pin completely.

Slide out the selector rails to remove the selector forks. When doing this, hold the selector forks so that they do not tilt and jam on the rails.

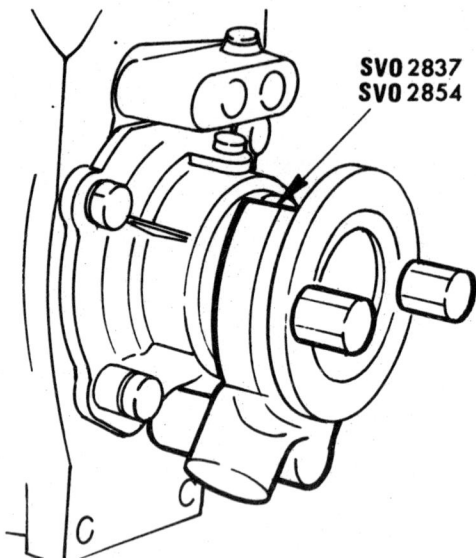

Fig. 34. — The special wrench required to hold the gearbox flange. Refer to Section 3.1.2. for details of the tool number required for various engines.

Unscrew the bolts securing the rear cover and turn the cover to clear the idler gear shaft. Drive out the idler gear shaft to the rear and let the idler gear fall to the bottom of the box. Pull out the main shaft.

Unscrew the screws from the cover over the input shaft and slide the cover along the shaft to remove it. Lever out the oil seal from the cover with a pointed tool (this seal should always be replaced when the box is dismantled).

Drive out the input shaft from the box. Remove the circlip and press off the bearing (only if necessary). Take the idler gear from the bottom of the box. Pull out the reverse gear shaft with puller SVO 2878. Remove the layshaft cluster.

Dismantling the main shaft: Dismantle as below according to the type of box:

With Overdrive: Remove the circlip and press off the rotor for the overdrive oil pump. Remove the circlip for

the main shaft bearing (rear) and slide the 1st/2nd speed
engaging sleeve forwards. Place the shaft under a press,
supporting under the 1st speed gear as shown in Fig. 35,
and press out the shaft.

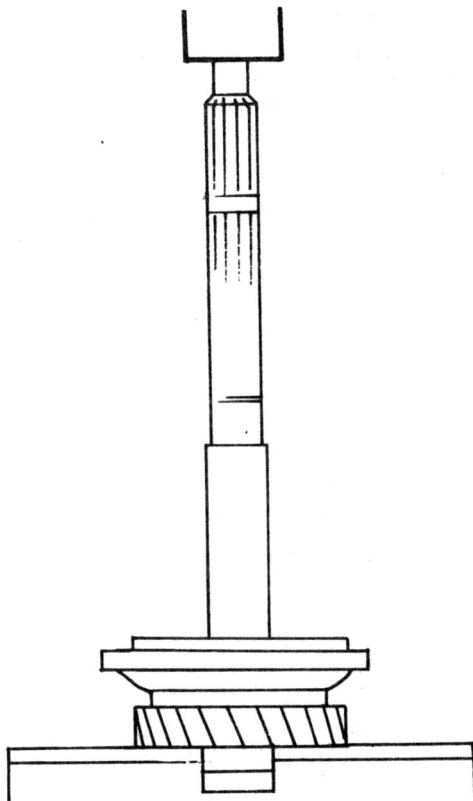

Fig. 35. – Dismantling the main shaft (M41, with overdrive).

Without Overdrive: Unscrew the flange nut and remove
the flange as already described in Section 3.1.2. Slide the
1st/2nd speed engaging sleeve fully forwards and place
the shaft under a press, supporting under the 1st speed
gear. Refer to Fig. 36 and press out the shaft with a
suitable drift.

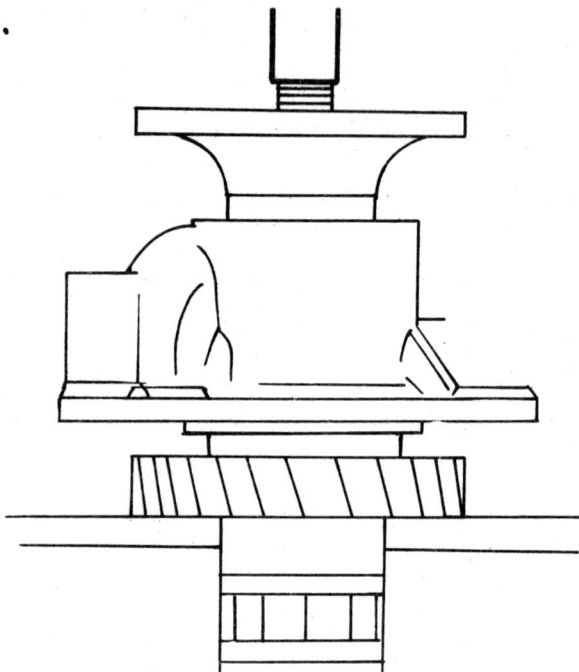

Fig. 36. — Dismantling the main shaft (M40, without overdrive).

For all main shafts, proceed as follows:

From the shaft remove these parts: baulk ring, thrust washer, operating sleeve, inserts and springs. Remove the circlip from the front end of the shaft. Use a two-arm puller and remove the synchroniser hub and 3rd speed gear from the shaft. Remove the thrust washer.

Remove the circlip and the thrust washer from the front of the 2nd speed gear and slide off the gear wheel, the baulk ring and the spring. Remove the oil seal from the rear cover and take out the speedometer gear. If necessary, remove the securing circlips and press out the ball bearing.

3.1.4.   INSPECTION

Clean all parts thoroughly in solvent and dry off with compressed air. If rags are used to clean and dry the components then make sure that they are not fluffy and shedding cotton or material; this is particularly important when dealing with a gearbox fitted with overdrive.

Inspect all parts and reject any that show signs of wear, scoring or damage. Having progressed this far with servicing of the gearbox it is simply not worthwhile to spoil the job by refitting parts that are not in first class condition.

Check all gear teeth for signs of scuffing, scoring or chipped teeth. Damaged or worn gears must be replaced as a pair. It is quite useless to attempt to mate a new gear with a worn one since they will not last for more than a few hours running.

Clean and inspect all bearings and replace any that show signs of wear, roughness, overheating or fretting (this latter is on the inner or outer diameters and shows as a black or brown marking that cannot be removed by the usual cleaning procedures).

Remember to clean out the main casing thoroughly.

The synchroniser cone surfaces must be free from scoring.

The two faces should seat firmly together under hand pressure.

3.1.5.   ASSEMBLY

Commence assembly with the main shaft, dealing with the units according to the type of box and as outlined below.

If the ball bearing has been removed from the rear cover, refit it using tool SVO 4080 and then fit the circlip.

There are different thicknesses of circlips available and the thickness must be selected so that it fits snugly into the groove.

Gearbox without Overdrive: Place the speedometer gear on the bearing in the rear cover. Press in the seal with drift SVO 2412 or some other drift of a suitable diameter.

Fit the parts for the 1st and 2nd speed synchronisers to the main shaft. Refer to Fig. 37 and make sure that the springs are fitted as shown (i.e. the ends of the springs and the gaps must not be in line at the front and back).

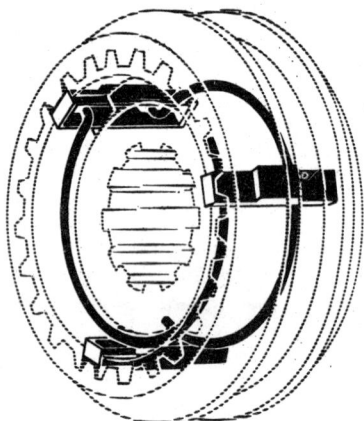

Fig. 37. — Assembling the synchroniser inserts and springs. Note that the spring gaps must be in different positions on each side.

Gearbox without Overdrive: Fit the synchroniser cone, the 1st speed gear and the thrust washer. Place the rear cover on the shaft, making sure that the speedometer gear is correctly positioned.

Fit the flange, then the washer and nut. These operations are the same as already described, using the same tools as mentioned in Section 3.1.2. Tighten the flange nut to a torque of 9.5 - 10.5 kgm (65 - 75 lb.ft.).

Gearbox with Overdrive: Place the rear cover and ball bearing onto a sleeve and fit the thrust washer, 1st speed gear and synchroniser cone and press in the shaft. Select a circlip of a suitable thickness to fit snugly into the groove. Fit the rotor for the oil pump, together with the key and circlip.

Fit the synchroniser cone, 3rd speed gear and thrust washer to the shaft and again select a circlip as before.

Fit the thrust washer, 3rd speed gear and synchroniser cone to the shaft. Assemble the 3rd/4th synchroniser parts correctly (refer to Fig. 37) and then fit the assembly to the main shaft. Again select a circlip of the proper thickness.

For all boxes, assemble as follows:

Fit the striker lever and striker. Fit the reverse gear and reverse shaft, noting that the shaft must project outside the housing as shown in Fig. 38.

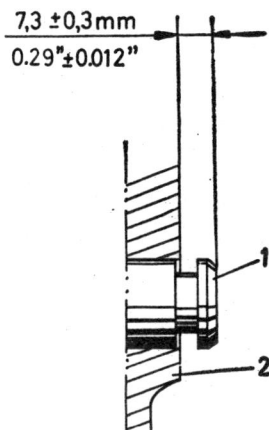

Fig. 38. — Fitting dimension for the reverse shaft in the gearbox housing.

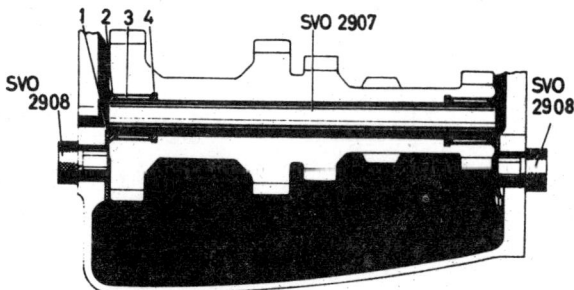

Fig. 39. — Initial assembly of the layshaft cluster with the dummy shaft in position.

1.	Thrust washer	3.	Needle bearing
2.	Spacer washer	4.	Spacer washer

73

Refer to Fig. 39 for assembly of the layshaft. Place the dummy mandrel SVO 2907 in position and fit the needles to each end (24 to each bearing; use grease to hold the needles in position). Fit the spacing washers, again using grease to hold them in position. Use the centring plugs SVO 2908 to guide the washers and position the layshaft assembly in the bottom of the box.

Input Shaft: Press the bearing to the input shaft by using sleeve SVO 2412 as shown in Fig. 40. Select a circlip of suitable thickness and fit it to the shaft so that it fits the groove snugly.

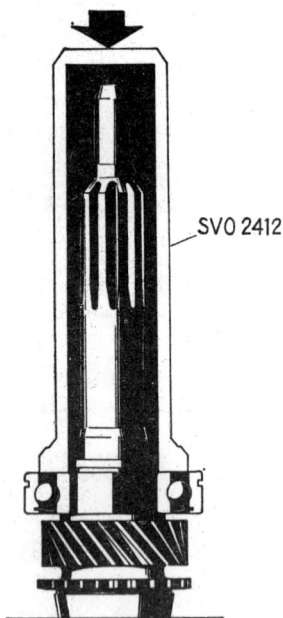

SVO 2412

Fig. 40. — Fitting the bearing onto the input shaft.

Fit 24 greased needle rollers into the input shaft and press the shaft into the housing. Fit the oil seal into the cover with drift SVO 2867. Fit the cover over the input shaft and secure to the housing.

IMPORTANT! Later and current covers use "O" rings as seals for the bolts. Do not forget to refit these if they were there originally.

Place the main shaft into the housing and turn the gearbox so that the layshaft shaft can be fitted from the rear. Fit the shaft while holding the dummy shaft and gradually push it out with the proper shaft. Take care that the thrust washers do not move out of position during this operation.

Gearbox without Overdrive: Fit the bolts for the rear cover.

Gearbox with Overdrive: Fit the overdrive unit, using new locking washers for the intermediate flange.

Fit the selector rails and forks in the reverse sequence to removal. When fitting the securing pin (a new one) move the selector fork to the rear position so that the pin can be inserted into the shaft.

NOTE: If the end caps at the front end of the housing have been removed then these should be fitted so that the centre end cap projects about 4 mm (0.16 in.) as shown by the "A" dimension in Fig. 41.

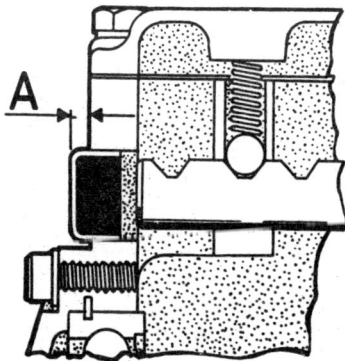

Fig. 41. — Fitting the end cap over the selector rail. The "A" dimension should be approx. 4 mm (0.16 in.).

Finally refit the interlock ball and springs and fit the gearbox cover. Check that all gears engage and disengage smoothly without interference. Install the gearbox as already described.

3.2. Overdrive

3.2.0. DESCRIPTION

The overdrive unit is of the epicyclic gear type and attached to the rear end of the gearbox. The overdrive is engaged by an electrical solenoid actuating a hydraulic valve. The overdrive can only be engaged when the main gearbox is in 4th (top) speed since there is a contact on the gearbox cover that is only closed when in top gear.

3.2.1. TECHNICAL DATA

Type:	*M 41 (M 40 gearbox with overdrive)*
Reduction Ratio, Overdrive:	
1973 models:	*0.797 : 1*
Earlier models:	*0.756 : 1*
Oil Pressure:	
Direct drive:	*Approx. 21 psi*
Overdrive:	*455 - 500 psi*
Lubricant:	*Engine oil SAE 30 or Multigrade SAE 20W/40*
Capacity, gearbox and overdrive:	*1.6 litres (2.8 Imp. pints, 3.4 U.S. pints)*

3.2.2. OVERDRIVE — SERVICING (IN VEHICLE)

Certain operations and checks can be made with the overdrive still in the vehicle and these are detailed below.

CAUTION! The oil in a vehicle that has just completed a run may be at a high temperature, take care that it does not cause burning when draining or disconnecting parts of the oil system.

Oil Pressure Checks: The oil pressures can be checked with the vehicle on test rollers or when being driven. The checks can also be made with the rear wheels jacked up but this is not recommended for reasons of safety. Remove the plug under the operating valve and connect pressure gauge SVO 2834. Check to the following values:

—   At 40 kph (25 mph) in direct drive the oil pressure should be about 1.5 kg/sq.cm (21 psi).

—   Engage the overdrive at the same speed and check that the pressure rises to 32 - 35 kg/sq.cm (455 - 500 psi).

—   Disengage the overdrive and check that the pressure drops to the first value in not more than 3 seconds.

Solenoid and Operating Valve: This is a single unit and replaced as such. Use a 25 mm spanner to remove. Use a new seal and "O" ring when refitting. Tighten to 4.2 - 5.5 kgm (30 - 40 lb.ft.).

Checking and Replacing the Relief Valve: Remove the base plate and pre-filter and collect the oil (do not forget the previous warning). Remove the plug under the valve (tool SVO 2836) and dismantle the piston, springs and retainer and other parts. Wash all parts and inspect carefully. The following parts are available as spares: End washer, cylinder, small piston, adjuster washer, low pressure spring, large piston, plug and "O" rings.

Assemble by using new "O" rings. Tighten the plug to a torque of 2.2 kgm (16 lb.ft.). Use a new gasket to the pre-filter and base plate.

Cleaning Orifice Nozzle: The nozzle is accessible after the relief valve cylinder has been removed. Clean with compressed air only.

Check Valve: Clean and inspect all parts and replace as necessary. Tighten the plug to a torque of 2.2 kgm (16 lb.ft.).

Filter: The filter should be cleaned in white spirit and blown dry with compressed air. Fit a new seal to the plug and tighten to 2.2 kgm (16 lb.ft.).

After any of the above operations refill with oil and check for leaks.

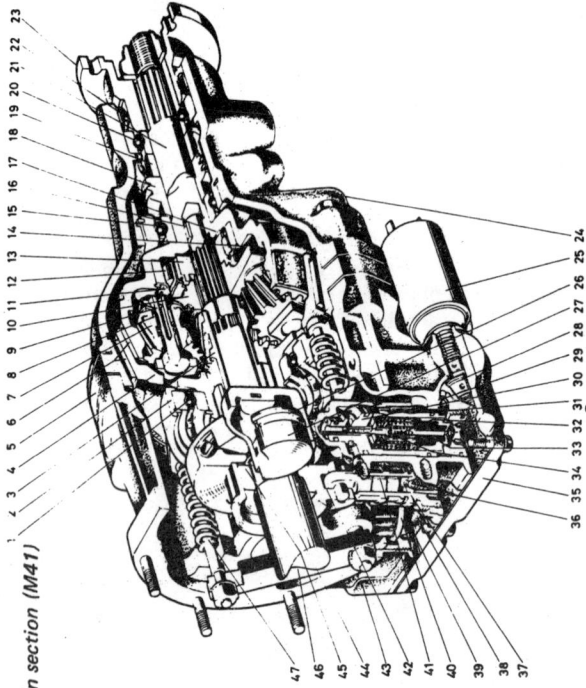

Fig. 42. -- The overdrive unit in section (M41)

1. ⎫ Thrust bearing and
2. ⎬ retainer
3. Sun wheel
4. Clutch sliding member
5. Brake ring
6. Clutch linings
7. Planet gear
8. Needle bearing
9. Shaft
10. Planet carrier
11. Oil thrower
12. ⎫ Uni-directional clutch
13. ⎬ rollers and clutch
14. Oil trap
15. Bearing
16. Bush
17. Thrust washer
18. Speedometer gear
19. Spacer
20. Bearing
21. Output shaft
22. Oil seal
23. Coupling flange
24. Rear casing

25. Solenoid
26. ⎫ Piston seal and piston
27. ⎬
28. Operating valve
29. Orifice nozzle
30. ⎫ Cylinder top and
31. ⎬ cylinder
32. Spring
33. ⎫ Pistons, large
34. ⎬ and small
35. Base plate
36. Check valve, oil pump
37. Pump cylinder
38. Magnetic plug
39. Pre-filter
40. Fine filter
41. Pump plunger
42. Connecting rod
43. Front casing
44. Input shaft (gearbox
   main shaft)
45. Eccentric
46. Bridge piece
47. Spring

3.2.3. REMOVING THE OVERDRIVE

If the overdrive is to be removed from the vehicle with the main gearbox remaining in the car, then first drive the vehicle with the overdrive engaged and then disengage the overdrive with the clutch pedal DEPRESSED. This will avoid any residual torsion which might make it difficult to remove the unit from the gearbox.

The overdrive is quite simple to remove on its own. Follow the previous general instructions and disconnect the solenoid cable and the bolts securing the overdrive unit to the intermediate flange. Pull the overdrive unit backwards until it comes free from the gearbox main shaft.

3.2.4. DISMANTLING

It is not recommended that the overdrive unit should be stripped unless the reader is confident that he can meet the requirements already outlined. Absolute cleanliness is essential when working on the unit and all traces of dirt, dust and other contamination must be removed from the components and casings before assembly.

3.3. Automatic Transmission

3.3.0. TECHNICAL DATA

Make:	*Borg-Warner*
General type identification:	*Type 35*
Type to Engine Designation:	
B20 A:	*327*
B20 B:	*325*
B20 E:	*321*
B20 F:	*351 H*
Reduction Ratios (x Convertor Ratio):	
1st:	*2.31 : 1*
2nd:	*1.45 : 1*
3rd:	*1 : 1*
Reverse:	*2.09 : 1*
Size of convertor:	*240 mm (9.5 in.)*
Torque ratio in convertor:	*2 : 1 to 1 : 1*
Weight, with fluid:	*53.1 kg (117 lb.)*
Fluid type:	*Automatic Transmission Fluid Type F*

Fluid capacity:	*6.4 litres (11.4 Imp. pints, 13.5 U.S. pints)*
Normal operating fluid temperature:	*Approx. 110 - 115° C*

3.3.1.   REMOVAL AND INSTALLATION

Before commencing removal of the automatic transmission, the reader is reminded of the very heavy weight
of the box and the need to provide for a trolley-type
jack of adequate size to carry the load.

Take off the oil dipstick and remove the filler pipe
clamp. Remove the bracket from the dashboard and the
throttle control cable. Disconnect the exhaust pipe at
the flange.

Jack up the vehicle and support with stands both front
and rear. Remove the drain plug and drain the oil.

CAUTION!   The oil will be very hot if the vehicle has
recently been driven for any distance.

Place lifting hook SVO 2727 in position as for gearbox
(manual) removal. Disconnect the propeller shaft from
the transmission flange. Disconnect the controls from the
selector shaft lever, also the reinforcing bracket under
the oil pan.

Unscrew the convertor attaching bolts one at a time by
rotating the crankshaft to gain access to each bolt.

Unscrew the rear engine mounting nut and remove the
crossmember. Disconnect the exhaust pipe bracket and
the mounting bracket. Remove the speedometer cable
from the box and release the oil filler pipe.

Lower the engine by about 20 mm (0.8 in.). Disconnect
the cables from the starter inhibitor and unscrew the
starter motor bolts.

Place a trolley-type jack in position, together with
fixture SVO 2746. Unscrew the convertor casing attachment bolts and pull the transmission backwards, at the
same time releasing the guide pin on the convertor.
Lower and remove the transmission.

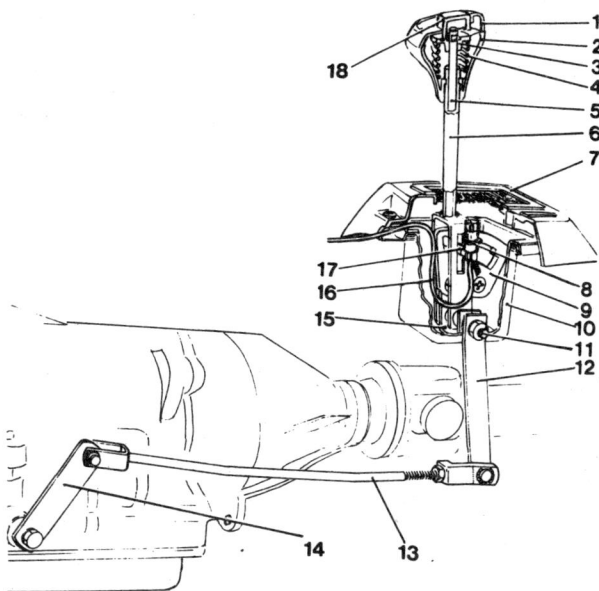

Fig. 43. — Automatic transmission, selector controls.

1.⎫ Selector lever, upper
2.⎭ and lower sections
3.⎫
4.⎭ Washer and spring
5. Push rod
6. Selector lever
7.⎫ Shift cover and shift
8.⎭ illumination lamp
9. Inhibitor plate
10. Housing
11.⎫
12.⎭ Shaft and lever
13. Control rod
14. Lever
15. Bracket
16. Lamp cable
17. Inhibitor
18. Button

Install the transmission in the reverse sequence to removal and refit the electrical cables. Refer to the section on selector controls for further information on setting.

3.3.2. ADJUSTING THE SELECTOR CONTROLS

To adjust the selector controls, refer to Figs. 43 and 44 and adjust as necessary to the following values:

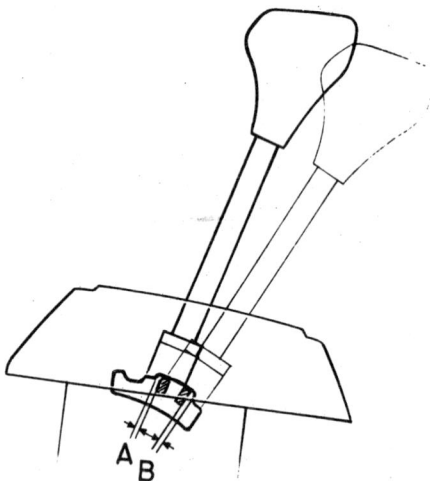

Fig. 44. – Automatic transmission, adjusting the selector lever.

If the shift rod has been disturbed the length should be set to 405 mm (16 in.) between the bolt centres of the clevises.

The clearance for the selector gating is shown in Fig. 44, at "A" and "B". In positions "D" and "2" the clearances should be the same in both positions, or a little greater in position "D", with a minimum of 1 mm (0.04 in.).

Check that there is still the same clearance with the selector at "1" and "P".

3.3.3. ADJUSTING THE THROTTLE CABLE

Check that the engine idling speed is correct and that the inner and outer cables are correctly attached. Screw up the threaded sleeve until it almost touches the stop (crimped on the cable) for single carburettor vehicles, or is 1 mm (0.39 in.) away for twin carburettor vehicles.

With the accelerator pedal fully depressed, check that the carburettor lever is in the fully open position on the stop and that the line pressure at convertor stall speed is at least 11 kg/sq.cm (160 psi). The stall speeds are:

B20 A engine:	2,200 rpm
B20 B engine:	2,100 rpm
B20 E engine:	2,550 rpm
B20 F engine:	2,450 rpm

If the transmission is still not satisfactory after this adjustment, it is recommended that it is serviced by a dealer since the full adjustment procedures involve the use of a tachometer and manometer.

3.3.4. FLUID CHECKING

Oil changing is normally only required after a major servicing or re-conditioning operation. The oil level should, however, be checked every 10,000 km (6,000 miles). Always have the vehicle on level ground and refer to the Owner's Handbook for the procedures to be adopted. Use only fluid of the recommended specification and never put any kind of additive into the system. If frequent topping up is required the transmission should receive immediate attention to discover and correct the fault causing the loss of oil.

3.4. Tightening Torque Values

Flange nut (M40 gearbox):	*9.5 - 10.5 kgm (65 - 75 lb.ft.)*
Flange nut (M41 with overdrive):	*11 - 14 kgm (80 - 100 lb.ft.)*
Automatic Transmission:	
Torque convertor drive plate:	*3.5 - 4.1 kgm (25 - 30 lb.ft.)*
Pressure point:	*0.6 - 0.7 kgm (4 - 5 lb.ft.)*
Drain plug:	*1.2 - 1.7 kgm (9 - 12 lb.ft.)*

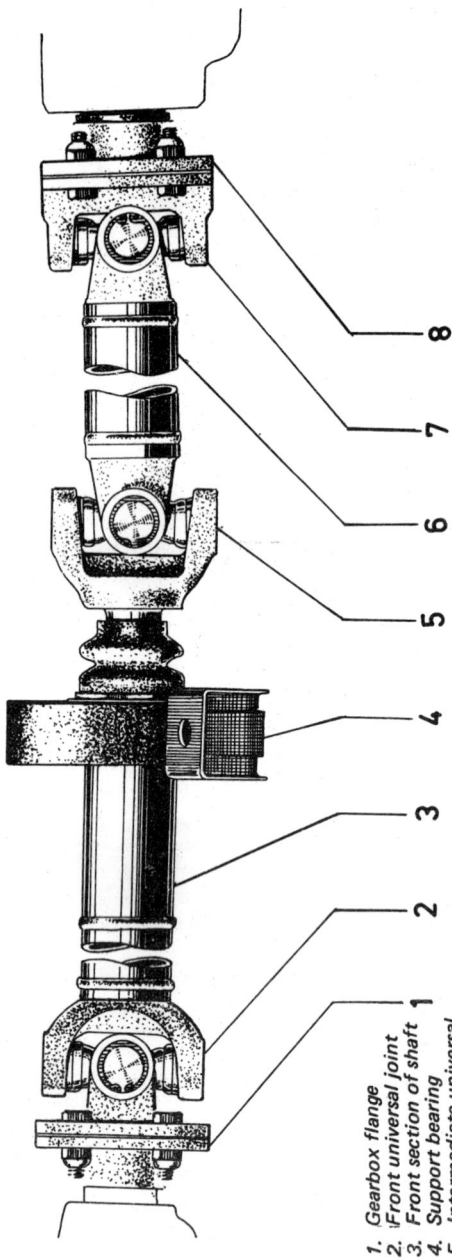

Fig. 45. — The propeller shaft and support bearing.

1. Gearbox flange
2. Front universal joint
3. Front section of shaft
4. Support bearing
5. Intermediate universal joint
6. } Rear shaft and
7. } universal joint
8. Rear axle flange

4.   PROPELLER SHAFT

4.0.   Technical Data

Type:	Tubular, divided, with three universal joints
Centre support bearing:	Sealed ball bearing in a flexible support
Shaft fixings:	Flanged either end
Spline lubrication:	MP grease with molybdenum disulphide
Universal joint lubrication:	Sealed, no routine greasing required
Run-out of shaft, max.:	0.25 mm (0.01 in.) on a dial indicator

4.1.   Removal and Installation

Jack up and support the vehicle on stands. A pit or garage type lift will give better access if available.

Remove the bolts from the front and rear flanges. Access to the bolts is rather restricted and the special sockets available will make it easier to carry out this operation.

Use tool SVO 2779 for vehicles with B20 A, B and F engines and SVO 2846 for the B20 E engine.

Loosen the cover for the support bearing and remove the complete shaft assembly. Note that the propeller shaft is factory-balanced and that all parts must be marked so that they can be replaced in the same positions. Take great care that the shaft is not subjected to rough treatment. Never hit the shaft with any metal tool and do not apply any undue force to the tube.

Install the shaft in the reverse sequence to removal.

4.2.   Servicing

4.2.0.   SHAFT AND UNIVERSAL JOINTS

Separate the front and rear assemblies at the spline joint. Bend back the lock washer at the centre bearing and unscrew the nut. Remove the rear section of the shaft and pull off the support bearing (refer to Fig. 46).

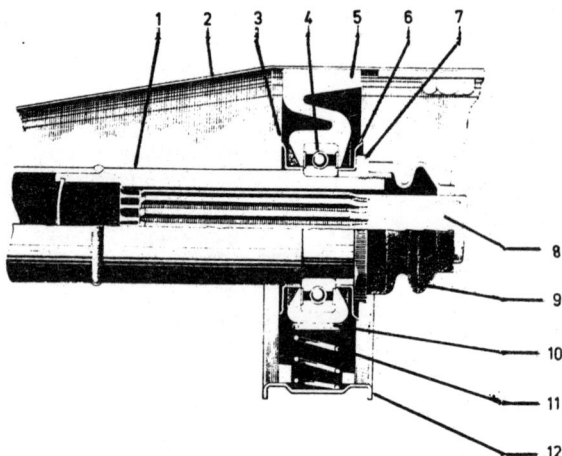

Fig. 46. — Sectional view of the propeller shaft support bearing.

1. Front section of shaft
2. Floor tunnel
3. Dust cover
4.\ Ball bearing and
5./ rubber housing
6. Dust cover
7. Nut
8. Rear section of shaft
9. Rubber gaiter
10.\ Washer and
11./ suspension spring
12. Cover

Secure the shaft in a vice with soft jaws, gripping as near the universal joint as possible. Remove the snap rings from the bearings and then carefully drive out the spider as far as it will go. The needle bearing will now be about halfway out and can be fully removed. Drive out the other side bearing in the same fashion and completely dismantle the joint.

Replace the needle bearings and spiders if worn or damaged. If the rubber seals are damaged they should not be re-used. Clean out the old bearings if they are to be re-used. Use multi-purpose grease and only fill the bearing about half full of grease.

To install the universal joint bearings, first insert the spider and push it over to allow the bearing to be inserted. Fit new snap rings to the yokes.

4.2.1. SUPPORT BEARING

Note that the support bearing can be removed and replaced, if necessary, without removing the front flange bolts or the front section of the shaft. Pull off the complete support bearing as already described. Press the old bearing from the rubber housing and fit the new bearing.

Fit the support bearing and the other parts. Inspect the splined joint and if it appears dry, lubricate with MP grease mixed with molybdenum disulphite. On no account attempt to completely fill the female spline section. There should only be a generous smear of grease to the splines and no more.

5. FRONT AXLE AND FRONT SUSPENSION

5.0. Description

The Volvo 140 series has an independent front suspension, all of which is mounted onto a box-section front axle member. At each end of the member are coil springs and shock absorbers, together with upper and lower control arms of the wishbone type. The steering knuckle is carried in ball joints at the upper and lower control arms and the inner pivot of the control arms is made with rubber bushes.

The front wheels are carried on a stub axle fitted with a pair of taper roller bearings to each hub.

The ball joints are sealed and require no routine lubrication. The rubber seals should be inspected every 20,000 km (12,000 miles) and replaced if necessary.

5.1. Technical Data

NOTE: The data given below is for current vehicles (1973). If the vehicle being serviced is an earlier type with one of the B18 engines you are recommended to consult your dealer or distributor with precise details of the model and year to ensure that the correct spares are obtained.

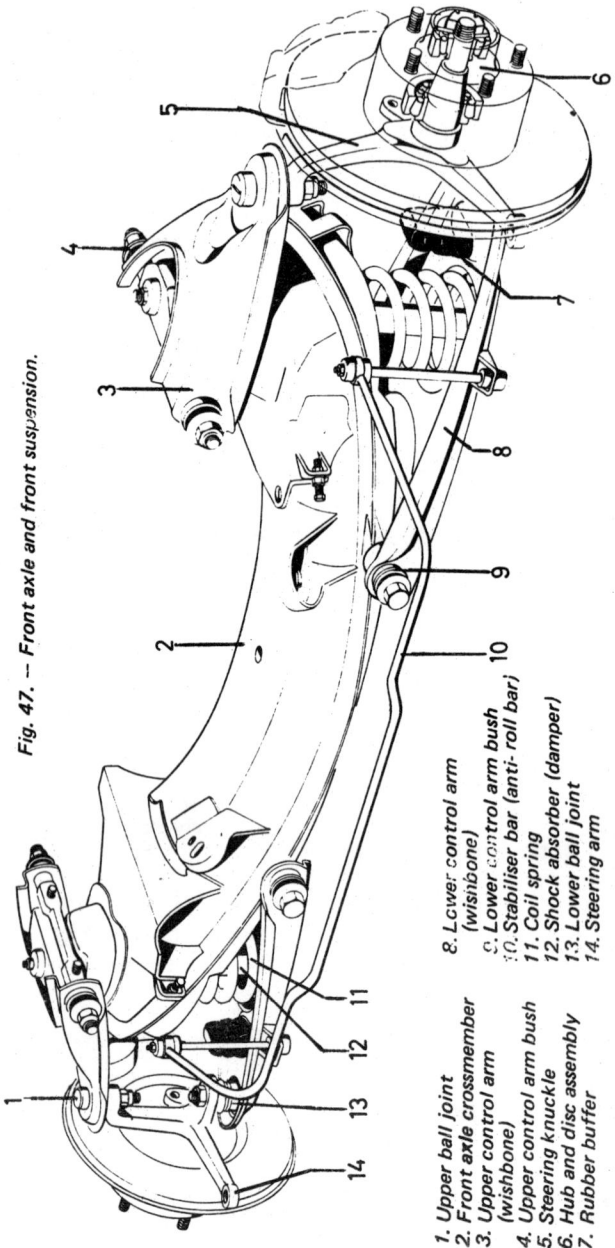

Fig. 47. — Front axle and front suspension.

1. Upper ball joint
2. Front axle crossmember
3. Upper control arm (wishbone)
4. Upper control arm bush
5. Steering knuckle
6. Hub and disc assembly
7. Rubber buffer
8. Lower control arm (wishbone)
9. Lower control arm bush
10. Stabiliser bar (anti-roll bar)
11. Coil spring
12. Shock absorber (damper)
13. Lower ball joint
14. Steering arm

Front wheel bearings:	Taper roller
Shock absorbers:	Double-acting, hydraulic, telescopic
Front springs:	Coil type

Spring Data:	
Wire diameter:	15 mm (0.59 in.)
Outer diameter:	126 mm (4.96 in.)
Total turns:	8.7
Load at length of 195.5 mm (7.7 in.):	1,188 - 1,254 lb.

5.2.   Front Hubs and Bearings

5.2.0.   REMOVAL AND INSTALLATION

With the front wheel removed, detach the front brake assembly as described in the section on the brakes.

Remove the grease cap from the hub and withdraw and discard the split pin. Unscrew the hub nut and pull off the hub with remover SVO 2726. Remove the inner bearing cone from the stub axle with tool SVO 2722. Drift out the inner and outer bearing cups from the hub.

Fit a new seal to the stub axle. Fit it carefully and make sure that the "A" dimension (see Fig. 48) is 14 $\pm$ 0.5 mm (0.55 $\pm$ 0.02 in.).

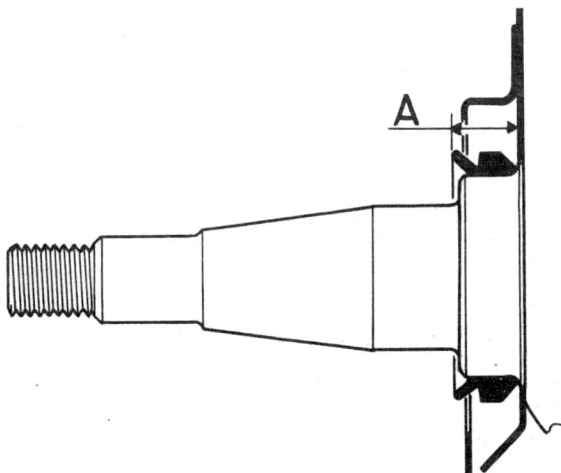

Fig. 48. — Fitting the front stub axle seal. The dimension "A" must be 14 mm/0.55 in. ($\pm$ 0.5 mm/0.02 in.).

Refer to the next section for bearing assembly and adjustment.

5.2.1.   WHEEL BEARING – FITTING AND ADJUSTMENT

Clean out all old grease from the hub and grease cap. Inspect the bearings for wear, scoring or signs of over-heating and replace as necessary. Remove all grease from the disc with a de-greasing solvent.

Use a good quality wheel bearing grease for the bearings.

Pack the bearing rollers and cages with grease, working it well into the cages. Apply grease to the recess between the bearings and to the grease cup. The grease should come to about the level of the outer race bores but on no account attempt to fill the cavities completely.

Press on the bearing cups with a suitable drift and make sure that they are fully seated against the shoulders.

Fit the bearing, the washer and the castle nut and tighten the nut gradually while "rubbing" the hub back and forth to seat the bearings and rollers. Tighten the hub nut to 7 kgm (50 lb.ft.) and then slacken the nut by 30º and see if a slot in the nut coincides with the split pin hole. If the split pin hole and a slot are not in line then slacken the nut just far enough to allow the two to be aligned.

Check that the wheel rotates freely and then insert and bend over a new split pin.

Complete the assembly of the brakes and wheel.

5.3.   Front Suspension

5.3.0.   FRONT END COMPLETE – REMOVAL AND INSTALLATION

Jack up the vehicle under the front jack attachment points at each side, using jacks of adequate size for the job.

Remove the front wheels and position a hoist so that the front of the engine can be lifted to take the weight off the front engine mountings. Disconnect the steering arms from the steering rods and remove the brake hoses from the brackets. Remove the stabiliser bar brackets.

Remove the lower nuts from the engine front mountings. Support the front end with a trolley jack and remove the attachment bolts. Lower and remove the complete front end unit.

To install the front end, first fit guide pins to the front bolt holes and raise the assembly into position. Fit the rear bolts with plastic plugs and then remove the guide pins and fit the two remaining bolts. Refit the remaining parts in the reverse sequence to removal.

5.3.1.   STEERING KNUCKLE — REMOVAL AND INSTALLATION

Remove the front brake unit and the hub as already explained. Remove the steering rod ball joint with tool SVO 2294.

Take the load off the lower control arm with a jack and slacken the ball joint nuts a little. Loosen the ball joints and remove the steering knuckle.

Install in the reverse sequence to removal, making sure that the ball joints do not twist as the nuts are tightened. Install the hub and brake components as already described.

5.3.2.   UPPER BALL JOINTS

The upper ball joint of the control arm is removed with tools SVO 2699 and 2701 as shown in Fig. 49.

Jack up the vehicle as before and remove the road wheel. Slacken the ball joint nut and tap the joint until it loosens. Remove the nut and suspend the upper end of the arm to avoid straining of the brake hose. Lift up the control arm slightly and remove the joint with the tools as shown in the illustration.

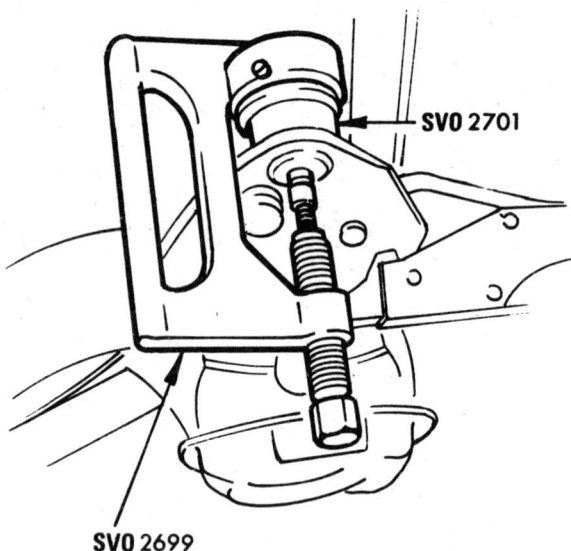

SVO 2701

SVO 2699

Fig. 49. — Removal of the front suspension upper ball joint.

Install the ball joint after checking for wear and that there is sufficient grease in the cover. Fit the joint by using the same tools plus the sleeve SVO 2704. Make sure that the recess of the joint (the small slot in the outer diameter) is in line with the longitudinal axis of the control arm (within about $\pm 8^o$). Tighten the ball joint, making sure that the pin does not rotate.

Refit the remaining parts as before.

5.3.3.   LOWER BALL JOINTS

There are two types of ball joint, one with an internal spring and one without a spring. To make a quick check on the possible wear of the joint (with the joint in position and a normally laden vehicle) refer to Fig. 50. This illustration shows the Type 2 joint, with spring, and the dimension "A" should not exceed 113 mm (4.5 in.). The joint without a spring (Type 1) does not have the conical extension to the bottom end and the maximum overall dimension should not be more than 99.3 mm (3.91 in.). If the length of the joint is more than the

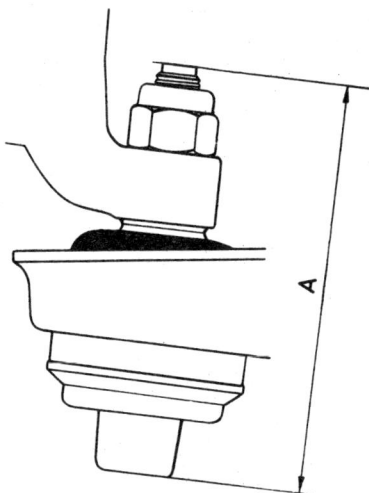

Fig. 50. — Type 2 lower ball joint (with spring). Note that there are two types of ball joint and each has a maximum "A" dimension which is dealt with in Section 5.3.3.

specified dimension then the component must be replaced.

Remove the ball joint with tools SVO 2700 and 2699. The tools for installation are SVO 2699, 2701 and 2703.

5.3.4. UPPER CONTROL ARM — REMOVAL AND INSTALLATION

Carry out the operations already described to remove the upper ball joint. Remove the bolts of the control arm in a similar fashion to that shown by Fig. 68. Take off the shims carefully and keep them in a safe place in their proper order.

Install in the reverse sequence to removal, noting the following points:

The control arm is secured with a special locking screw with a nylon insert. Replace the screw if the locking pad is damaged or worn. Fit the shims in the same position as they were before.

Tighten the nuts for the control arm shaft to 5.5 - 6.2 kgm (40 - 45 lb.ft.). Check the castor and camber as detailed in Section 6.6.2.

5.3.5. UPPER CONTROL ARM — SERVICING

The upper control arm is shown in Fig. 51. Bushes should be removed and replaced in accordance with the following notes:

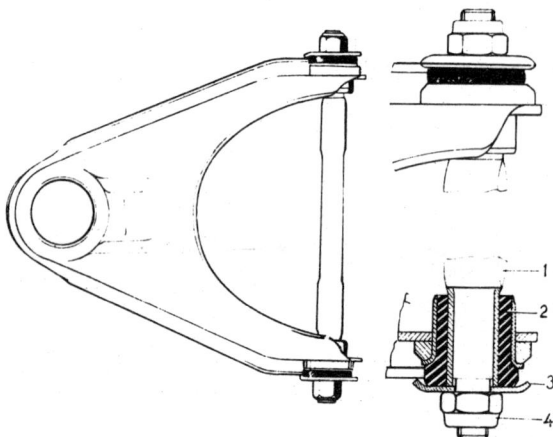

Fig. 51. — Details of the upper control arm (wishbone).

1.	Control arm shaft
2.	Bush
3.	Washer
4.	Nut

Remove the nuts and washers to release the control arm shaft. Fix the arm securely into a vice fitted with soft jaws and carefully bend out the arm ends so that the "C" washer spacer (SVO 2729) can be fitted. Drive out one of the bushes with tool SVO 2729 and a hide hammer. Remove the other bush in a similar way.

Install the new bushes with tools SVO 2699, 2702 and 2706. Make sure that the shaft fits the recess of tool 2702.

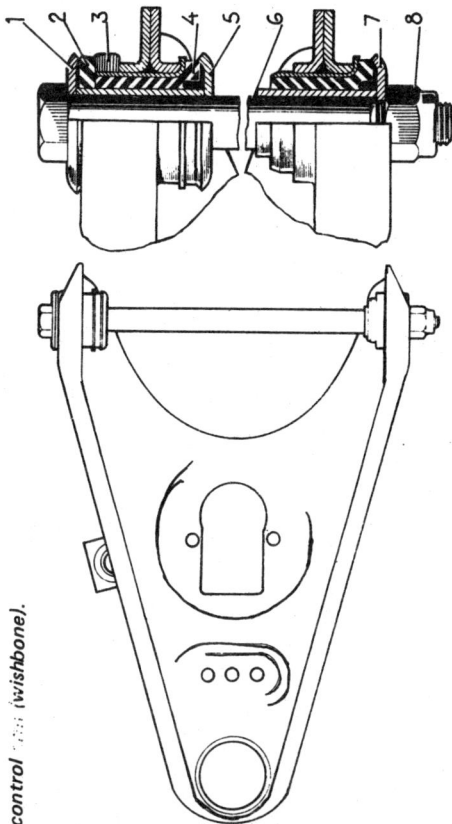

Fig. 52. — Details of the lower control arm (wishbone).

1. Washer
2. Rubber ring
3. Spacer ring
4. Bush
5. Washer
6. Control arm shaft
7. Washer
8. Nut

5.3.6. LOWER CONTROL ARM — REMOVAL AND INSTALLATION

The lower control arm is shown in Fig. 52. To remove, jack up the vehicle and remove the road wheel as before. Take off the shock absorber, disconnect the steering rod from the arm and remove the stabiliser attachment.

Place a jack beneath the control arm and remove the steering knuckle assembly. Lower the jack and remove the spring.

Remove the nut from the control arm and take the unit away from the vehicle.

Install in the reverse sequence to removal. Tighten the nut for the shaft with the control arm in a horizontal position.

5.3.7. LOWER CONTROL ARM — SERVICING

When replacing the bushes it must be remembered that there are special bushes for vehicles with radial ply tyres and these are different to those used with cross-ply tyres.

Remove the bushes as shown in Fig. 53. Tools SVO 2699 and 2701 are used. The bush marked "A" in the illustration is numbered 2905 for radial ply tyres and 2904 for cross-ply tyres.

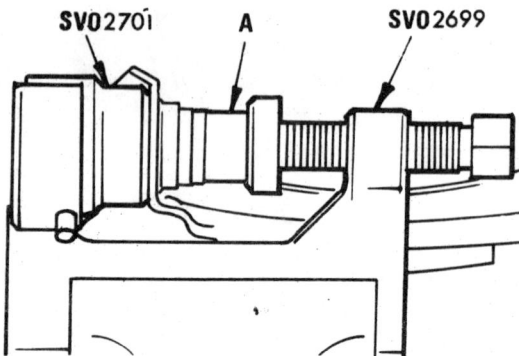

Fig. 53. — Removing the bush of the lower control arm. Note that sleeve "A" is different for radial and cross-ply tyres. The bush is also different (refer to Section 5.3.7.).

Note that bushes for radial ply tyres must be fitted so that the recess is at the 90° angle (± 5°) as shown in Fig. 54.

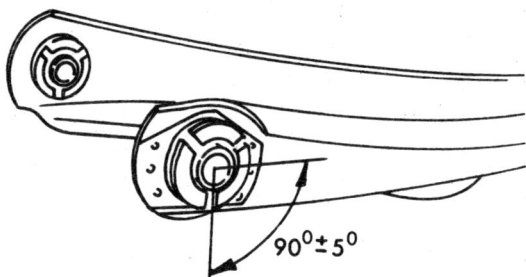

$$90° \pm 5°$$

Fig. 54. — The lower control arm bush for radial tyres. The recess must be at the angle shown.

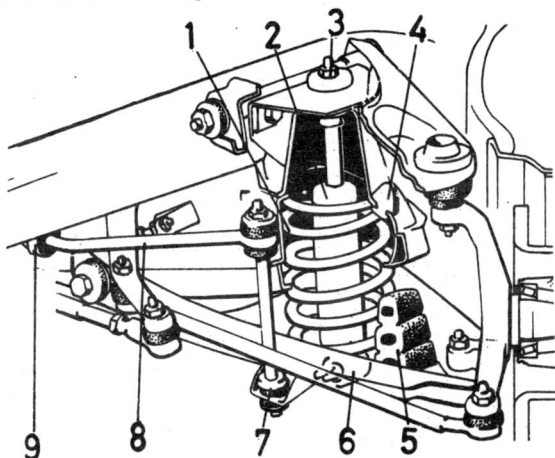

Fig. 55. — Detailed view of the front spring and shock absorber components.

1.	Spring
2.	Shock absorber (damper)
3.	Shock absorber upper attachment
4.} 5.}	Rubber buffers
6.	Shock absorber lower attachment
7.	Stabiliser (anti-roll) bar attachment
8.	Stabiliser bar (anti-roll bar)
9.	Stabiliser bar, chassis attachment

5.4. Coil Springs and Shock Absorbers

5.4.0. FRONT SPRINGS — REMOVAL AND INSTALLATION

A detailed view of the coil spring and shock absorber is shown in Fig. 55.

Follow the previous instructions regarding removal of the ball joint nuts, brake hoses and so on and note the following points:

Remove the shock absorber top and bottom mountings. Lower and lift the control arm (lower) with a jack immediately under the spring.

Inspect the springs carefully and replace if worn, cracked or weak. Inspect and replace the bump rubbers if damaged or deteriorated.

5.4.1. SHOCK ABSORBERS

The shock absorbers are sealed units and cannot be dismantled. If the unit does not function satisfactorily in both directions, or if the lower fixed rubber bushes are damaged, the complete unit should be replaced. A rough check of the function can be made by noting the effect when rocking the car up and down, or by examining the effect when operating the unit on the bench. Note that the resistance of the shock absorber is about three times as great when it is extended as when it is compressed. This is as it should be and must not be mistaken for faulty operation.

To remove the shock absorber, take off the upper mounting first and then the lower. Refer to Fig. 56 and assemble the top mounting as shown. Note that the nut is tightened on assembly until it is in contact with the spacing sleeve.

5.5. Tightening Torque Values

Wheel nuts:	*10 - 14 kgm (70 - 100 lb.ft.)*
Steering knuckle nut:	*2.1 - 2.5 kgm (15 - 18 lb.ft.)*
Upper control arm shaft nut:	*5.5 - 6.2 kgm (40 - 45 lb.ft.)*

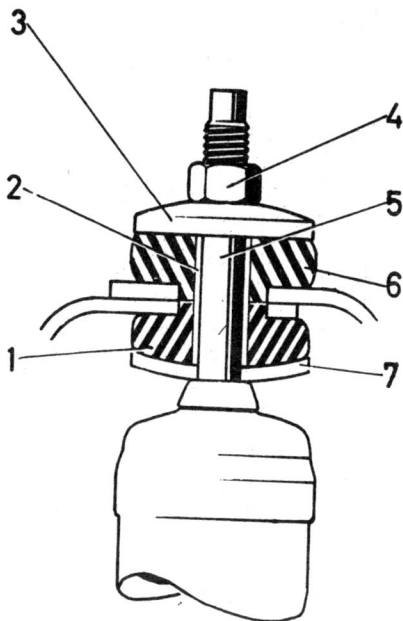

Fig. 56. — The front shock absorber upper attachment.

1.)	Rubber bush and
2.)	spacer sleeve
3.)	
4.)	Washer and nut
5.	Spindle
6.	Rubber bush
7.	Washer

Lower control arm shaft nut:	14 - 18 kgm (100 - 130 lb.ft.)
Upper control arm shaft bolt:	5.5 - 7.0 kgm (40 - 50 lb.ft.)
Upper ball joint nut:	8.5 - 10 kgm (60 - 70 lb.ft.)
Lower ball joint nut:	10 - 12 kgm (75 - 90 lb.ft.)

6.   STEERING

6.0.   Description

The steering gear for the Volvo 140 series vehicles may be either a conventional worm and roller type or a ZF ball nut type power steering unit.

The lower end of the steering column is fitted with a special "break-away" safety mechanism that prevents the column and wheel being forced forward in the event of a collision. The 1973 models have a smaller diameter steering wheel with a larger padded centre section than the earlier models but are otherwise the same.

The power steering unit is dealt with separately since it is a radically different unit to the conventional type. Power steering is, of course, an option that may not be fitted to all vehicles.

6.1.   Steering Box

6.1.0.   TECHNICAL DATA

Type:	*Cam and roller*
Steering ratio:	*17.5 : 1*
Ball joints, steering rod/	
tie rod:	*Sealed, no lubrication required*
Lubricant:	
Type:	*Hypoid oil*
Viscosity:	*SAE 80*
Capacity:	*0.25 litre (0.4 Imp. pint, 0.5 U.S. pint)*

6.1.1.   REMOVAL AND INSTALLATION

To remove the steering box, jack up and support the front of the car. Remove the two nuts from the flange at the bottom end of the column assembly and slacken the bolt clamping the serrations of the steering box shaft. Push the flange down towards the box as far as possible.

Remove the nut from the drop arm (Pitman arm) and pull off the arm with tool SVO 2370 or some other suitable puller. Remove the nuts and bolts securing the steering box and remove it from the vehicle.

To install the steering box, first fit the box into position and then proceed as follows:

Fit the drop arm so that the marks on the shaft and arm coincide. Set the steering wheel in the straight-ahead position and secure the two halves of the flange. Tighten the serration clamp bolt so that the distance between the steering housing and the flange is 27 ± 5 mm (1 ± 3/16 in.).

6.1.2. DISMANTLING AND INSPECTION

The steering box is shown in Fig. 57 and this illustration should be referred to when dismantling and assembling.

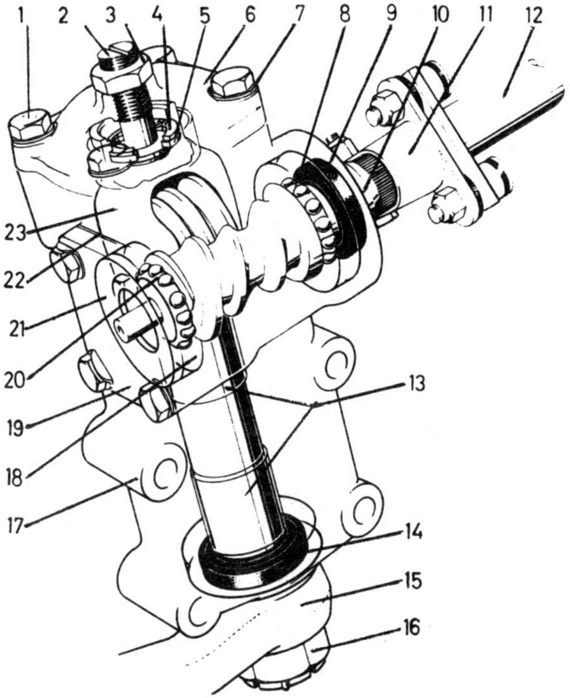

Fig. 57. — View of the steering gear.

1. Cover bolt
2. Adjusting screw
3. } Locknut and circlip
4. }
5. Adjusting washer
6. }
7. } Cover and tab washer
8. Upper ball bearing, worm shaft
9. Oil seal
10. Worm
11. Flange
12. Steering column lower section
13. Sector shaft bushes
14. Sector shaft oil seal
15. Drop arm (Pitman arm)
16. Nut
17. Steering housing
18. Worm shaft, lower bearing race
19. Worm end cover
20. Lower ball race
21. }
22. } Washer and spacer
23. Sector shaft (rocker shaft)

Mark the position of the flange and the shaft and then remove the flange. Place the steering gear in the centre position as shown in Fig. 58. Remove the upper cover (6, Fig. 57) and pull up the cover to allow the oil to drain.

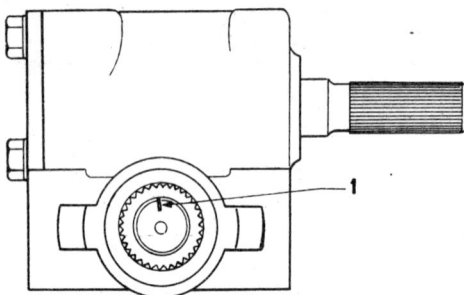

Fig. 58. — The steering unit with the mark (1) shown in the "centre" position.

Remove the cover and the sector shaft. Remove the lower cover (19), making sure that the spacers (22) are not mislaid.

Carefully tap the steering worm shaft so that the bearing outer races come free from the housing. Take out the worm with the bearings. Remove the locknut and screw from the cover. Remove the circlip from the sector shaft and remove the adjusting screw. Remove the sealing rings (9 and 14).

Wash all parts, discarding the gasket and the sealing rings.

Dry all components and the housing and inspect thoroughly, noting the following points:

—   Check the roller for wear, scoring and deep scratching and also the worm.

—   Check the sector arm shaft and bushes. Note that the bush in the cover cannot be replaced and the cover must, therefore, be replaced in the event of wear.

—   Replace scored or worn bearings.

6.1.3. SERVICING AND ASSEMBLY

Service the bushes and bearings as necessary, noting the following:

— Remove the outer bearing (upper) with drift SVO 2718 and handle 1801.

— Remove the bushes with SVO 2720 as shown in Fig. 59.

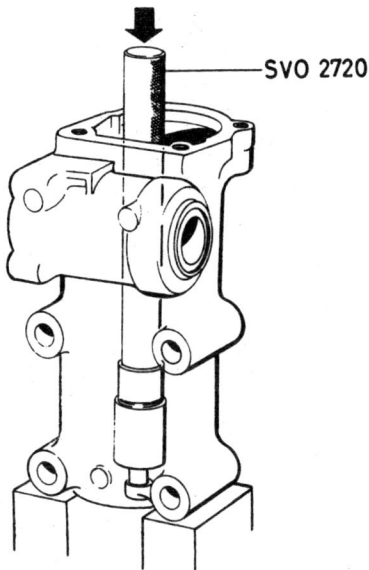

SVO 2720

Fig. 59. — Removing the bushes from the steering housing.

— Fit the sector shaft bushes with SVO 2716 and handle 1801. Ream the bushes with reamer and guide SVO 2254.

— Press in the upper outer bearing race with tool SVO 2717.

Fit the guide bolt with bearing into the housing, taking care that the sealing ring is not damaged. Fit the lower cover and washer with the shims as previously fitted.

Coat the two through bolts with non-hardening sealer and tighten the cover. Remove or add shims to give a torque on the shaft of 1 - 2.5 kgm (7.2 - 18 lb.ft.) as shown in Fig. 60.

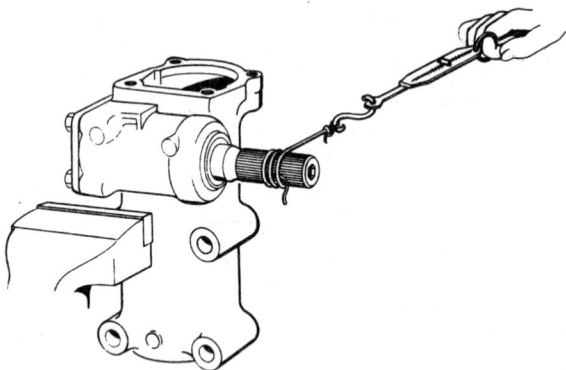

Fig. 60. — Checking the starting torque of the steering worm shaft.

Fit the adjusting screw, washer and lock ring to the sector shaft. Set the axial play of the adjusting screw by changing the washer thickness, aiming for as little play as possible (the screw must still rotate easily) but not exceeding 0.05 mm (0.002 in.).

Lubricate and fit the sector shaft together with the cover and gasket and tighten the bolts.

Fit the sector shaft oil seal with SVO 2719 or a suitable drift.

Locate the steering gear in the central position as before and adjust the screw so that the starting torque can be checked as in Fig. 61.

With a 210 mm (8.25 in.) long bar attached to the shaft the torque should be adjusted to 8 - 14 kg (18 - 31 lb.). Re-check the value after the stop nut has been tightened.

Fill the box with the specified amount of lubricant. Refit the flange in accordance with the matching marks previously made.

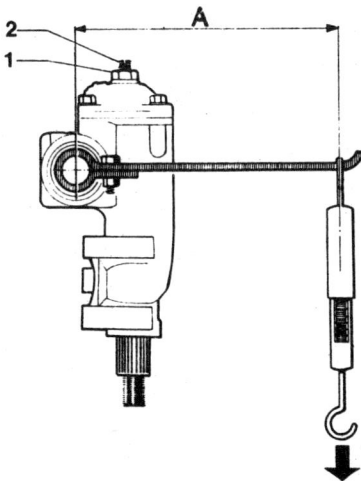

Fig. 61. — Checking the load of the assembled cam and roller.

A. 210 mm (8.25 in.) long bar
1. Locknut
2. Adjusting screw

6.2. Steering Rods and Tie Rod

The steering gear components are shown in Fig. 62. Note that ball joints cannot be adjusted or dismantled and must be replaced if faulty.

The steering rod ball joints are made in one with the steering rod. Note that the steering rods are marked "L" and "R" to indicate left-hand and right-hand sides (the marked ends should be fitted to the steering knuckle).

Remove the tie rod ball joints with tool SVO 2294 or some other similar puller. Unscrew the ball joint, noting the number of turns to disengage and replace the new part to the same position.

Adjust the toe-in after working on the rods or joints.

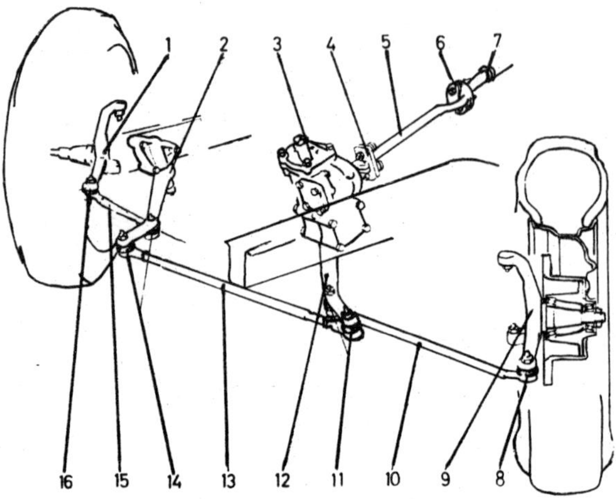

Fig. 62. — The steering gear components.

1. Steering knuckle, right
2. Relay arm
3. Steering box
4. Lower steering column flange
5. Lower steering column section
6. Upper steering column flange
7. Upper steering column section
8. Ball joint
9. Steering knuckle, left
10. Steering rod, left
11. Ball joint
12. Drop arm (Pitman arm)
13. Tie rod
14. Ball joint
15. Steering rod, right
16. Ball joint

6.3. Relay Arm

The relay arm assembly is shown in Fig. 63. Remove the complete relay arm assembly from the vehicle for servicing of the bush. Remove the bush as shown in Fig. 64. For insertion of the bush use a similar set-up but replace SVO 2734 with 2735.

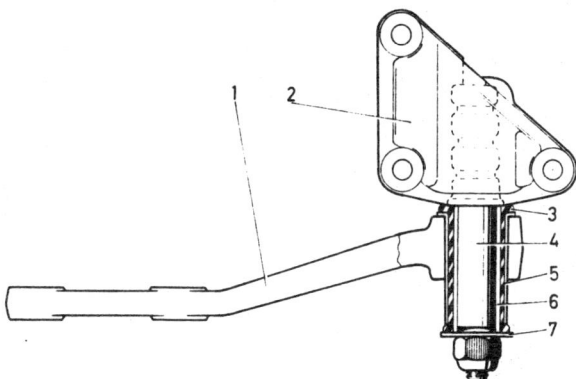

Fig. 63. — The relay arm assembly.

1.   Relay arm
2.   Bracket
3.   Rubber bush
4.   Bearing shaft
5.   }
6.   } Sleeves
7.   Washer

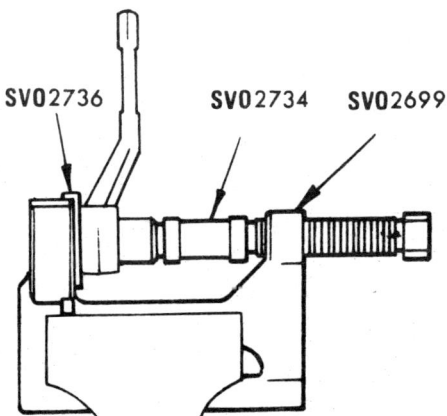

Fig. 64. — Removing the rubber bush from the relay arm. Insertion of the new bush is similar, except that SVO 2734 is replaced by 2735.

6.4. Power Steering

6.4.0. TECHNICAL DATA

Make and type:	*ZF. Ball-nut type*
Reduction ratio:	*15.7 : 1*
Lock-to-lock:	*3.7 turns*
Lubricant:	*Automatic Transmission Fluid type A or Dexron*
Lubricant capacity:	*Approx. 1.2 litres (2.1 Imp. pints, 2.5 U.S. pints)*
Power Pump:	
Make and type:	*ZF. Vane type*
Max. pressure:	*75 $\pm$ 5 kg/sq.cm (1066 $\pm$ 71 psi)*
Drive:	*Belt driven (1 : 1 to engine)*
Drive belt tension:	*About 5 mm (0.187 in.) deflection with the fingers midway between the pulleys*

6.4.1. GENERAL NOTES

The power steering unit and its drive are shown in Fig. 65. It is most important that the utmost cleanliness is observed whenever any part of the hydraulic system is disconnected. Always clean the parts BEFORE disconnecting any pipework.

Due to the complex nature of the units involved it is not recommended that dismantling or adjustment is attempted by the owner. It is preferable to have this work carried out by a dealer or distributor.

Note that the construction of the steering unit differs for LHD and RHD vehicles and this must be remembered if obtaining replacements or spares.

6.4.2. OIL CHECKING AND SYSTEM BLEEDING

Check the oil level every 10,000 km (6,000 miles). Note that with a stationary engine the oil level should be about 5 - 10 mm (0.2 - 0.4 in.) ABOVE the filler level mark. Fill with oil only with the engine stopped.

Drain the oil as follows:

Jack up the front of the car and remove the drain plug.

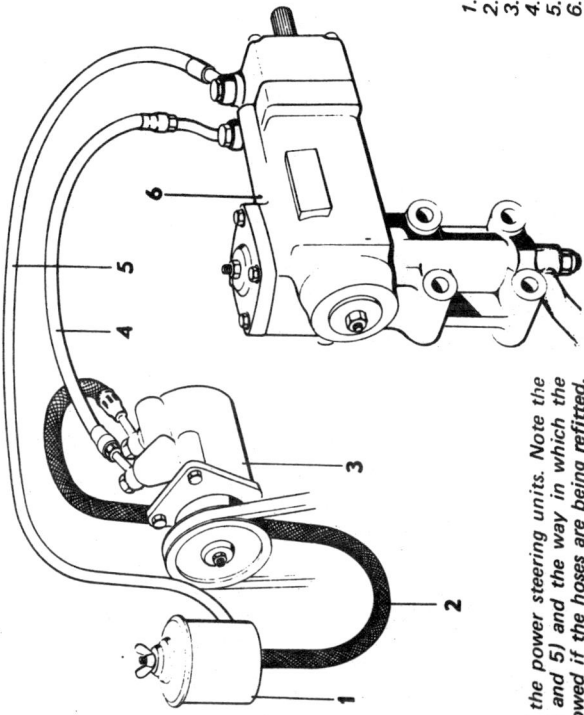

Fig. 65. — Arrangement of the power steering units. Note the connection of the hoses (4 and 5) and the way in which the hoses lay; this must be followed if the hoses are being refitted.

1. Oil reservoir with filter
2. Pump suction line
3. Power pump
4. Delivery oil line
5. Return oil line
6. Steering unit

Turn the steering wheel to left lock position and remove the reservoir cover. Start the engine and run for 10 seconds maximum. Turn the steering wheel gently from lock-to-lock and wait for all oil to drain.

Refilling and Bleeding: Do not re-use drained oil. Fill the reservoir to the edge of the container. Start the engine and add oil until the level stabilises. Slowly turn the wheel from lock to lock, add more oil if necessary.

Open the bleeder screw (top cover) by about half a turn and turn the wheel gently until oil flows out and then re-tighten. Continue turning the wheel until the fluid in the reservoir is free from most of the air bubbles.

Stop the engine and watch the oil level. If it rises more than 5 - 10 mm then there must be further air still in the system and bleeding must continue. Note that a small amount of air bubbles will probably remain in the reservoir but these will eventually disappear with running.

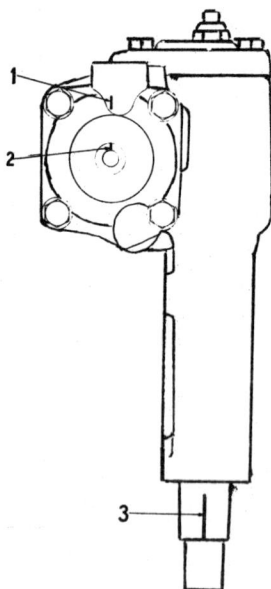

Fig. 66. -- The power steering housing set in the centre position as shown by marks 1, 2 and 3.

6.4.3. REMOVAL AND INSTALLATION

Removal of the power steering box follows the same procedures as for the conventional box. Drain the oil first and make sure that the connections are cleaned before removal and that all pipes and connections are blocked off to prevent dirt entering.

Install with the steering gear in the centre position as shown by the three marks in Fig. 66. The steering wheel and the road wheels should be in the straight-ahead position. Check that the distance between the steering housing and the lower flange is 12 ± 3 mm.

Fill with oil and bleed as in the last section.

6.5. Steering Column and Wheel

The steering column assembly is shown in Fig. 67. It should be noted that the upper bearing can be replaced if necessary but if the lower bearing is damaged the steering must be replaced complete.

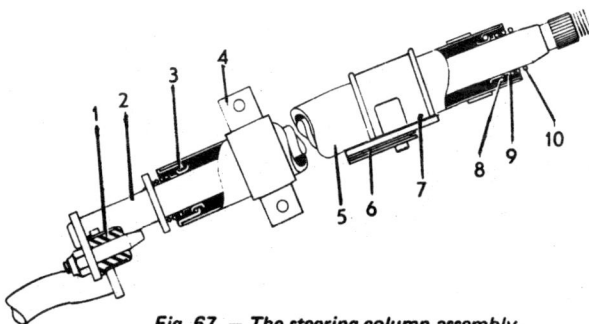

Fig. 67. — The steering column assembly.

1. Safety "break-away" feature
2. Upper column section
3. Lower bearing
4. Lower attachment
5. Steering column jacket
6. Upper attachment
7. Steering wheel lock
8. Upper bearing
9.
10. } Seat and spring

To remove the steering wheel, take off the attachment screws for the upper part of the direction indicator switch housing and lift off the housing. Remove the steering wheel nut and set the wheels to the straight-ahead position. Use puller SVO 5003 to remove the wheel.

Install in the reverse sequence, tightening the steering wheel nut to 3 - 4 kgm (20 - 30 lb.ft.). To replace the upper bearing, proceed as already outlined and pull out the spring and seat. Grease the new bearing with MP grease and refit the parts.

6.6. Wheel Alignment

6.6.0. TECHNICAL DATA

Castor:	
With B20 engines:	$+1^o$ to $+2^o$ (1973 models)
With B18 engines:	0° to 1°
Camber:	0° to $+0.5^o$
Toe-In:	
With B20 engines:	2 - 5 mm (0.08 - 0.20 in.)
With B18 engines:	0 - 4 mm (0 - 0.157 in.)
King pin inclination:	7.5^o
Turning angles:	At 20° of the outer wheel the inner wheel turns 21.5 - 23.5^o
Adjusting shim thickness:	0.15, 0.50, 1.0, 3 and 6 mm

6.6.1. WHEEL ALIGNMENT PRE-CHECKS

Before adjusting or checking the wheel alignment the following points must be correct and without play or wear if appropriate:

1) Tyre pressure and tyre wear.
2) Wheel rim run-out not more than 2.5 mm (0.1 in.).
3) Steering rods, arms, relay arm and tie rod.
4) Shock absorbers and coil springs.
5) Steering unit.
6) The vehicle must be unladen.

6.6.2. CASTOR AND CAMBER

Castor and camber should be adjusted at the same time. To adjust, slacken the special bolts at the upper control arm shaft as shown in Fig. 68. Use tool SVO 2713 and slacken the bolts by several turns.

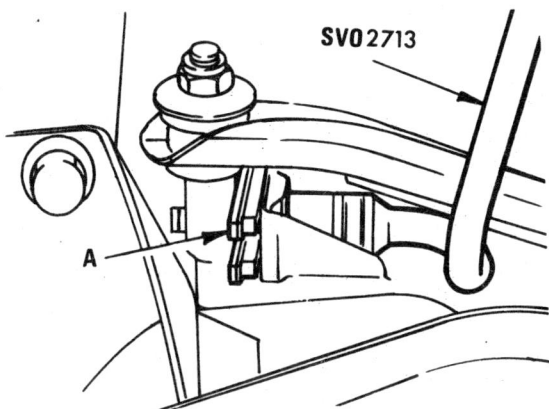

Fig. 68. — Adjusting the castor and camber by means of the shims (A). Note the special cranked wrench which is double-ended to reach both front and rear bolts.

Positive castor is obtained by ADDING shims to the REAR bolt or REMOVING shims at the FRONT bolt.

To maintain the camber it is necessary to keep the total shim thickness the same; in other words, to take shims from one side and add to the other side.

When the adjustment has been completed, tighten the bolts to 5.5 - 7 kgm (40 - 50 lb.ft.).

Camber is adjusted at the same shims, in this case the shim thickness being increased or decreased equally for both bolts. More "positive" camber is obtained by REMOVING shims and "negative" camber by IN-CREASING the shim thickness.

Shim thicknesses are listed in Section 6.6.0.

6.6.3.   TOE-IN

Toe-in should only be adjusted after the castor and camber have been set. The toe-in values are given in Section 6.6.0. and adjustment is made by alteration of the length of the tie rod centre tube. Slacken the lock-nuts on the tie rod and turn the rod in the required direction. Toe-in is increased by turning the track rod in the normal direction of rotation of the road wheels. Tighten the locknuts to a torque of 7.5 - 9 kgm (55 - 65 lb.ft.).

6.6.4.   STEERING LIMIT STOPS

The turning of the wheels is limited by stop screws at the drop arm and at the relay arm. Adjust the stops if necessary so that the maximum angle that the wheel axis makes with the longitudinal centre line of the vehicle is, in each case:

Without power steering: $40 - 41^o$
With power steering: $38 - 39^o$

Check that the brake hoses are clear at full lock in each direction.

6.7.   Tightening Torque Values

Steering wheel nut:	*2.8 - 4.0 kgm (20 - 30 lb.ft.)*
Worm upper cover	
(Std. steering):	*1.7 - 2.1 kgm (13 - 15 lb.ft.)*
Drop arm (Pitman arm) nut:	*17 - 20 kgm(125 - 145 lb.ft.)*
Steering box and idler arm	
nut (mounting):	*3.5 - 4.0 kgm (25 - 30 lb.ft.)*
Locknut for tie rod:	*7.5 - 9.0 kgm (55 - 65 lb.ft.)*
Nut for steering rod:	
M10:	*3.2 - 3.7 kgm (23 - 27 lb.ft.)*
3/8 x 24 UNF:	*3.2 - 3.7 kgm (23 - 27 lb.ft.)*
7/16 x 20 UNF:	*4.8 - 6.2 kgm (35 - 45 lb.ft.)*
Wheel nut:	*10 - 14 kgm (70 - 100 lb.ft.)*

7.   REAR AXLE AND REAR SUSPENSION

7.0.   Description

The semi-floating rear axle is attached to the body through two longitudinal trailing arms with coil springs between the axle and the rear sidemembers. A transverse track bar (Panhard-type bar) prevents lateral movement of the axle in relation to the body.

Double-acting telescopic shock absorbers are fitted which require no maintenance and cannot be serviced.

The outer end of each drive shaft (half shaft) is carried in a special roller bearing with a controlled non-adjustable end float.

The final drive is of the hypoid gear type and is built-in to the rear axle housing with a rear access cover. The pinion shaft and the differential carrier are fitted with taper roller bearings. Gear backlash, differential bearing pre-load and pinion location and pre-load are all adjusted by the use of shims.

All vehicles in the Volvo 140 series use the same design of rear axle, suspension and final drive but there are differences in axle ratios, spring ratings and speedometer gear ratios dependent on the actual model and the year of manufacture. Since it is not possible to give technical data for each model in detail we recommend that owners of early vehicles should always provide their dealer or distributor with the vehicle serial number and year of manufacture before obtaining spares.

7.1.   Technical Data

REAR SPRINGS

Models 142 and 145 (Standard):

External diameter:	*127.1 mm (5 in.)*
Effective turns:	*8.9*
Wire diameter:	*12.1 mm (0.48 in.)*
Loading for compression of 10 mm (0.4 in.):	*35 - 37 lb.*

Models 145 HV and 145 SV	*145 HV*	*145 SV*
External diameter:	*127.9 mm (5.1 in.)*	*127 mm (5.0 in.)*
Effective turns:	*9.0*	*8.6*
Wire diameter:	*12.85 mm (0.51 in.)*	*13.10 mm (0.52 in.)*
Loading for compression of 10 mm (0.4 in.):	*43 - 47 lb.*	*51 - 54 lb.*

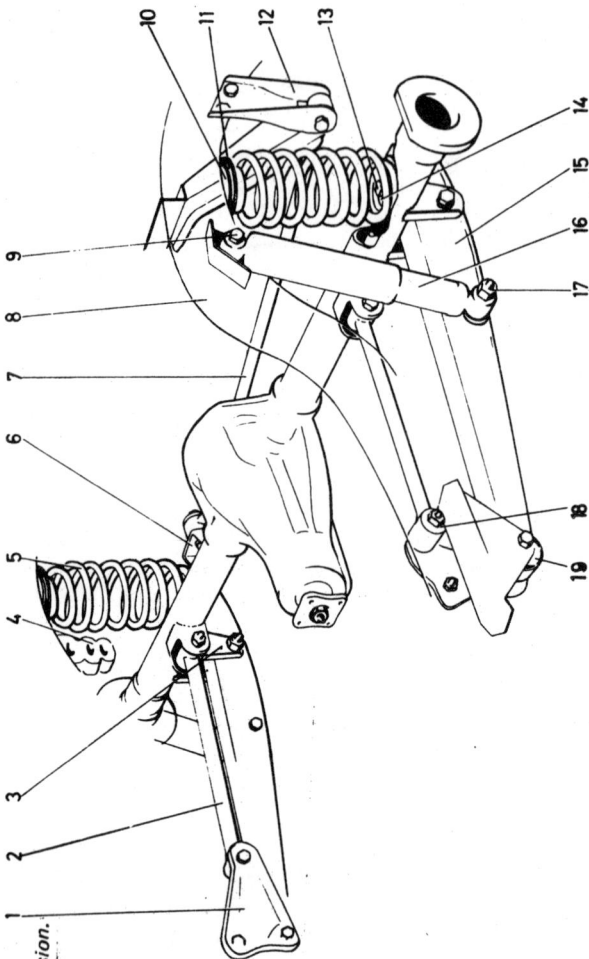

Fig. 69. — Rear axle and suspension.

1. Bracket
2. Support stay
3. Bracket
4. Rubber buffer
5. Rear coil spring
6. Bracket (track bar)
7. Track bar (Panhard type bar)
8. Rear sidemember
9. Shock absorber upper attachment
10.) Spring washer and
11.) spacer (rubber)
12. Bracket
13. Lower spring screw
14. Washer
15. Support arm
16. Shock absorber
17. Shock absorber lower attachment
18. Front support, stay attachment
19. Front bush, support arm

FINAL DRIVE

Final Drive Ratio (1973 Models):

142, 144 with M40 gearbox:	**4.10 : 1**
142, 144 and 145 with M40 or M41 gearbox:	**4.30 : 1**
142, 144 and 145 with automatic transmission:	**4.10 : 1**

Final drive ratio (early models):	**4.10 : 1 or 4.56 : 1**
Lubricant:	SAE 90 hypoid oil
Lubricant capacity:	1.3 litres (2.3 Imp. pints, 2.7 U.S. pints)
Run-out, crown wheel back face:	0.08 mm (0.0032 in.) max.
Backlash, crown wheel and pinion:	0.15 - 0.20 mm (0.003 - 0.008 in.)

Pinion Bearing Pre-Load:

New bearings:	11 - 23 kg/cm (9.55 - 20 lb.in.)
Used bearings:	6 - 11 kg/cm (5.21 - 9.55 lb.in.)

Differential bearing pre-load:	0.13 - 0.20 mm (0.005 - 0.008 in.)

7.2.   Rear Suspension

7.2.0.   REAR COIL SPRINGS — REMOVAL AND INSTALLATION

Jack up the rear of the car and place chocks on the front wheels. Fit an axle stand in front of the rear jacking attachment points as shown in Fig. 70. Remove the road wheel.

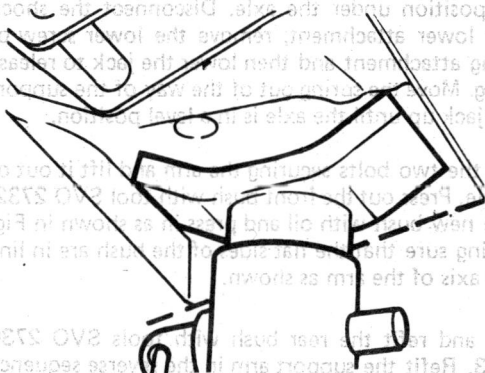

Fig. 70. — Locating the rear axle stand for work on the rear suspension and axle.

Jack up the rear axle so that the spring is compressed. Loosen the upper and lower spring attachments. Remove the upper attachment for the shock absorber. Carefully lower the axle jack and remove the spring from the vehicle when the load has been relieved.

To install the spring, fit the upper screw and washer inside the spring together with the spacer and washer (11 and 10, Fig. 69) and firmly secure the spring to the upper attachment. Raise the jack under the axle and fix the lower attachment of the spring with the washer and screw (14 and 13). Refit the shock absorber upper attachment and lower the axle jack.

7.2.1. SHOCK ABSORBERS — REMOVAL AND INSTALLATION

Raise and support the vehicle as in the previous section and remove the road wheel. Remove the shock absorber mountings by referring to Fig. 71.

When refitting the shock absorber, make sure that the spacer sleeve (2) is in position. The rear shock absorber cannot be dismantled or serviced.

7.2.2. SUSPENSION ARM — SERVICING

Raise the vehicle with axle stands as before and leave the jack in position under the axle. Disconnect the shock absorber lower attachment, remove the lower screw of the spring attachment and then lower the jack to release the spring. Move the spring out of the way of the support arm and jack up until the axle is in a level position.

Remove the two bolts securing the arm and lift it out of the vehicle. Press out the front bush with tool SVO 2732. Coat the new bush with oil and press in as shown in Fig. 72, making sure that the flat sides of the bush are in line with the axis of the arm as shown.

Remove and refit the rear bush with tools SVO 2730 and 2733. Refit the support arm in the reverse sequence to removal. Finally tighten the nuts for the arm bolts when the weight of the car is resting on its wheels.

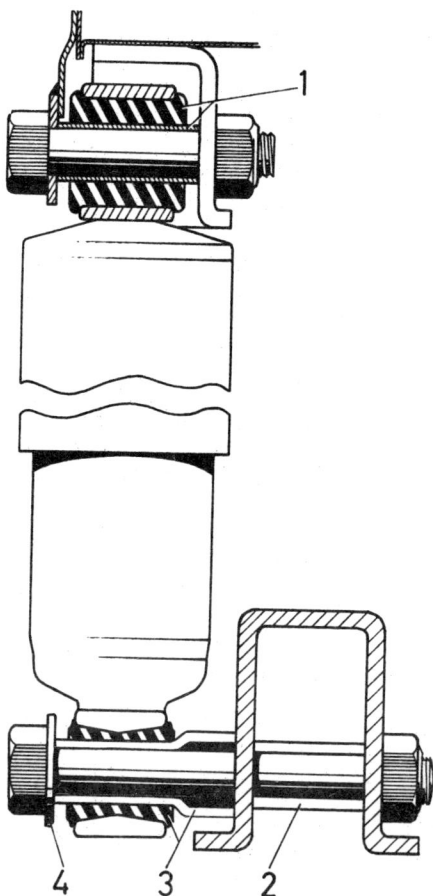

Fig. 71. — The rear shock absorber attachments.

1. Bush
2. Spacing sleeve
3. Bush
4. Washer

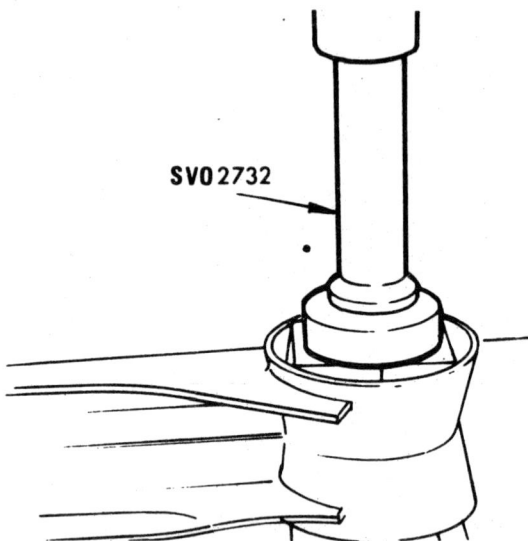

Fig. 72. — Removing and fitting the front bush in the support arm. Note the position of the flats in relation to the arm axis.

7.2.3. TRACK BAR AND SUPPORT STAY BUSHES

The track bar (Panhard bar) bushes and the support stay bushes (2, Fig. 69) can be replaced as follows:

Track Bar: Press out the small bushes with tool SVO 2730 and 2733. Replace the bushes with the same tools but reverse tool 2730. The large bushes are pressed out with tools SVO 2731 and 2733. Installation is with the same tools but with SVO 2731 reversed.

Support Stay Bushes: Use tools SVO 2734 and 2733. Coat the bush with oil before inserting and note that the marks on the bush must be at right angles to the rod as shown in Fig. 73.

7.3.   Drive Shaft and Wheel Bearing

The drive shaft (half shaft) and its bearing is shown in Fig. 74. Note that this is a special roller bearing that

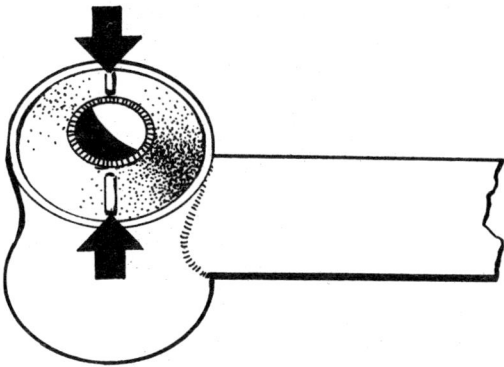

Fig. 73. — The position of the marks when fitting a support stay bush.

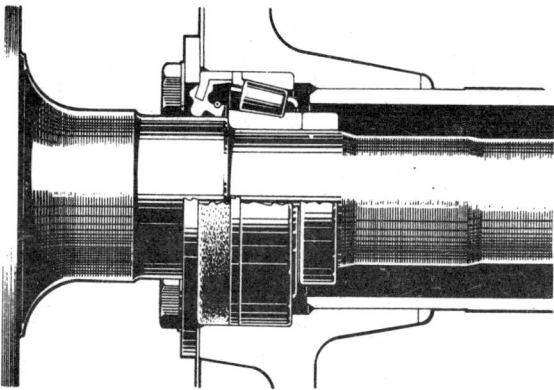

Fig. 74. — The rear axle, showing the special roller bearing and the oil seal.

incorporates a front ring to control end float which is pre-set and requires no adjustment.

It should also be noted that the bearing is retained by a rear collar that is a very tight fit on the shaft. Removal and installation of the bearing is best carried out with the special extractor and replacer and if these are not available the reader may decide to have the bearing replaced by a dealer.

If it is decided to carry out this work without the necessary tools then the retainer ring will have to be drilled and split and a new ring pressed on. On no account attempt to re-use the old retainer. Also take great care not to drill into or damage the axle shaft in any way.

To remove the drive shaft, chock the front wheels and support the rear on stands. Remove the road wheel and disconnect the brake hose from the caliper. Remove the brake disc and the brake unit, also disconnect the handbrake cable.

Insert a wrench through the holes in the drive shaft flange and remove the bolts securing the back plate and bearing retainer.

Pull out the drive shaft with tool SVO 2838 as shown in Fig. 75. In the absence of this tool it is recommended that a suitable tool is made up. On no account should the drive shaft be removed by hammering directly onto the flange.

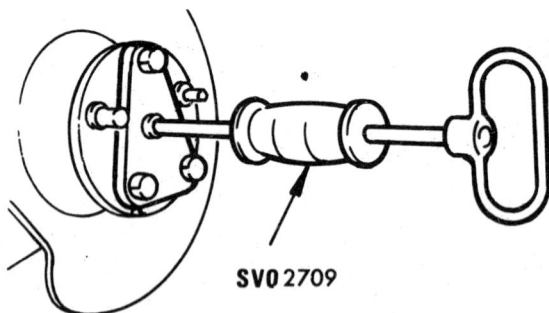

SVO 2709

Fig. 75. — Removing the rear axle drive shaft with the special tool and slide hammer.

Remove the bearing and retainer ring as shown in Fig. 75, using tool SVO 2838. Remove the oil seal and replace if necessary.

Fit the bearing with the same tool as for removal but this time add the fitting ring SVO 2839. Grease the seal lip

and the bearing before assembly and ALWAYS use a new
retainer ring.

Refit the drive shaft in the reverse sequence to removal.

Tighten the bearing retainer screws to a torque of 5 kgm
(36 lb.ft.).

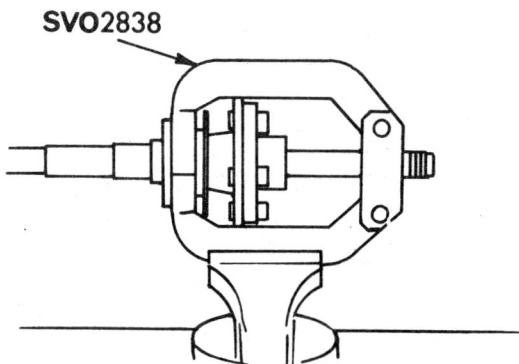

SVO2838

Fig. 76. — Removing the rear wheel bearing and retainer ring
with the special tool.

7.4.   Final Drive

7.4.0.   REPLACING THE PINION SHAFT OIL SEAL

The pinion shaft oil seal can be replaced without the
need to remove the axle from the vehicle. Disconnect
the propeller shaft at the rear flange and secure it out of
the way of the axle flange.

Remove the nut from the axle flange. To hold the flange,
use tool SVO 2854 for vehicles with B20 A, B or F
engines and SVO 2837 for B20 E engines.

Pull off the flange with tool SVO 2261 and remove the
oil seal with SVO 4030. Coat the oil seal lip with grease
and insert, using tool 2806. Tighten the flange nut to
28 - 30 kgm (200 - 220 lb.ft.).

7.4.1.   REAR AXLE — REMOVAL AND INSTALLATION

A trolley-type jack is to be preferred for removal of the rear axle, preferably fitted with a special fixture (SVO 2714) which supports the rear axle beneath the differential housing and at each side, around the axle tubes. If this equipment is not available then make sure that the axle is well secured to the jack so that it will not slip.

Chock the front wheels and place the rear on axle stands at the points shown in Fig. 70 (note that the stands must not be further forward than the dotted line in the illustration).

Remove the rear wheels and take out the shock absorber top bolts. Disconnect the handbrake cables from the levers and brackets. Remove the propeller shaft rear flange bolts and take off the brake pipe union from the axle casing. Remove the spring lower attachment bolts and then the attachments for the suspension arms, support stays and track bar. Lower the axle carefully and withdraw in a forward direction.

Install in the reverse sequence to removal. Adjust the handbrake and bleed the brake system. Refill with specified lubricant.

7.4.2.   FINAL DRIVE — DISMANTLING AND INSPECTION

It is important to remember that the assembly and adjustment of the final drive can only be properly carried out if the necessary tools and gauges are available. This is particularly important if the gears or bearings are to be replaced since the full checking procedures will then have to be carried out to position and pre-load the components in the proper way.

Axle stand SVO 2522 is recommended for all work on the final drive since the unit will otherwise be difficult to clamp. In the absence of the proper fixture it is suggested that a simple fixture be made up that will clamp on the casing tubes at either side of the final drive casing. If this fixture can be made so that it can rotate then this will further ease the handling problem.

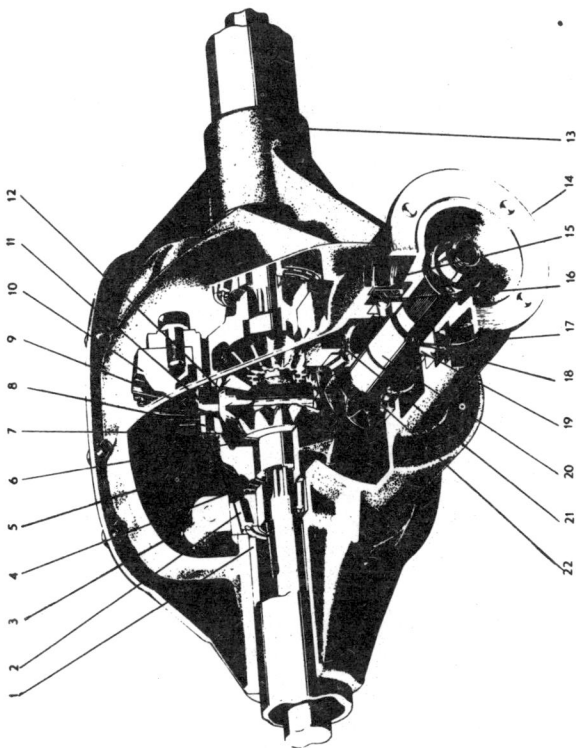

Fig. 77. – The final drive unit and differential.

1. Tubular axle casing
2. Differential carrier bearing
3. Bearing cap
4. Shims, carrier assembly
5. Differential carrier
6. Thrust washers, side gears
7. Differential side gear
8. Lock pin for shaft
9. Differential pinion
10. Crown wheel
11. Shaft, differential gears
12. Thrust washer
13. Rear axle casing
14. Drive flange
15. Dust cover plate
16. Oil slinger
17. Oil seal
18. Shims, bearing pre-load
19. Front pinion shaft bearing
20. Pinion shaft
21. Rear pinion shaft bearing
22. Shims, pinion position

125

Pull out the drive shaft and remove all other parts still attached to the axle. Remove the inspection cover and drain the oil. Clean the crown wheel and pinion and, before dismantling, check the tooth contact pattern.

Refer to Fig. 77 for an illustration of the final drive. Remove the bearing caps, adding marks for identification if none are there already.

Fit tool SVO 2394 and retainers 2601 as shown in Fig. 78. Tension the bolt until the tool fits exactly into the holes in the casing. Now tension the bolt by a further 3 - 3 1/2 turns and lift out the differential carrier assembly.

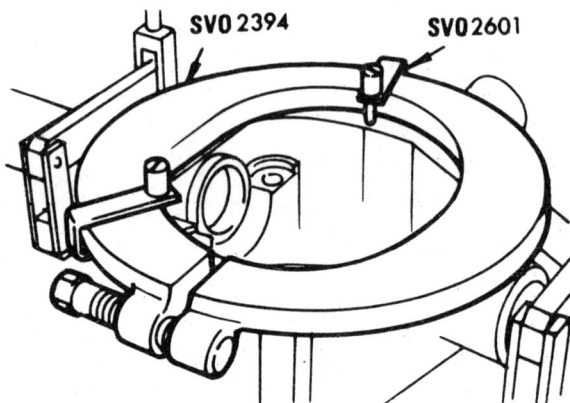

Fig. 78. — Expanding the casing to remove or assemble the differential carrier and bearings. The special tool is used for this operation. On no account attempt to carry out this operation in any other way.

Dismantle the pinion shaft flange and bearings. Remove the bearing cone behind the pinion with tool SVO 2392 as shown in Fig. 79.

Thoroughly clean the surface where the rear cover sits and remove any burrs. Dismantle the differential carrier parts. Loosen the crown wheel bolts and remove the gear. Drive out the lock pin for the differential shaft (from the back side of the crown wheel flange). Tap out the differential shaft and remove the block, gears and thrust washers. Pull off the differential carrier bearings with SVO 2483, taking care not to lose the shims.

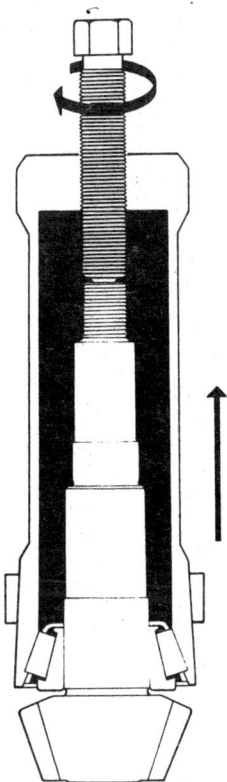

Fig. 79. — The collet-type tool used to remove the pinion shaft bearing cone (tool SVO 2392).

Clean all parts thoroughly and inspect. All damaged bearings must be replaced. Check all gears for wear or tooth damage. Refit the differential gears in a clean and dry condition and check the gear backlash with a dial gauge to one of the tooth flanks. If the play exceeds 0.06 mm (0.0024 in.) then select a thicker thrust washer. These are available in nine thicknesses, from 0.74 mm (0.029 in.) to 0.98 mm (0.039 in.) in steps of 0.04 mm (0.0016 in.).

Replace the pinion shaft oil seal as a matter of routine but note that this is not refitted until all checks have been carried out.

Discard the pinion nut if the nut has been removed more than twice. Make sure that the casing is not distorted or cracked.

7.4.3. ASSEMBLY AND ADJUSTMENT

Keep all parts as clean as possible when assembling. Oil all the rotating parts before assembly. It is important that the checking procedures are carried out in the order that they are described.

Differential Carrier: Place the side gears in position and then "roll" in the differential pinions with the thrust washers. Drive in the shaft and re-check the gear play. Fit the lock pin when the gear play is correct.

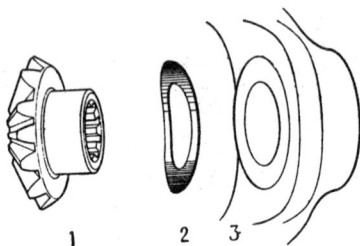

Fig. 80. — Fitting the differential gear thrust washer (2). Note the direction of the cone of the washer.

Fit the crown wheel, making sure that both clamp surfaces are clean and free from burrs. Use new bolts for those gears that are only locked by the friction of the threads. Tighten the bolts to a torque of 6.5 - 9 kgm (45 - 60 lb.ft.).

Pinion Shaft: Fit the adjusting ring SVO 2685 and tool 2841 to the pinion as shown in Fig. 81. Place the ring in the carrier so that the screw faces the inside of the casing.

The pinion height is now to be adjusted so that the distance from the head of the pinion to the centre line of the differential carrier bores is 2.55 in. It is important to note that the unit may be "Volvo" manufactured or

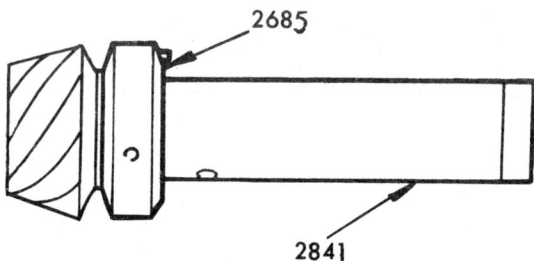

Fig. 81. — The pinion shaft assembled with the adjuster ring and ready for checking of the pinion height when placed in the housing.

made by a sub-contractor. Volvo units are identified by the figure stamped or etched on the pinion head having no plus or minus sign while others always have either a plus or minus sign (these values are in 1/100 mm units).

To check the pinion position, set up the equipment as shown in Fig. 82 (tools SVO 2284, 2393, 2685 and 2684). The check is carried out by measuring, with the dial gauge, the readings shown by the indicator on the diameter of tool 2393 and the then on the top face of setting block (also 2393). The height of the pinion is set by rotating the adjuster ring (2685) as follows:

If a Volvo unit is fitted then the top of the gauge should always be BELOW the height set by the adjuster. For other units the two heights will be the same if the pinion head is marked "0". If the pinion is marked "minus" then the gauge should be HIGHER than the adjuster and if the pinion is marked "plus" then the gauge should be LOWER than the adjuster. If, for example, a Volvo unit pinion is marked "33" then the gauge should lie 0.33 mm BELOW the adjuster dimension.

To establish the dimension, first set the dial gauge plunger to the diameter of the shaft and set to zero. Move the indicator across to the gauge head and read off the difference in height. Adjust the ring to bring the dimension to the correct value and then lock with the screw.

Remove the tools and the pinion and place the pre-set adjusting ring in the measuring fixture as shown in Fig.

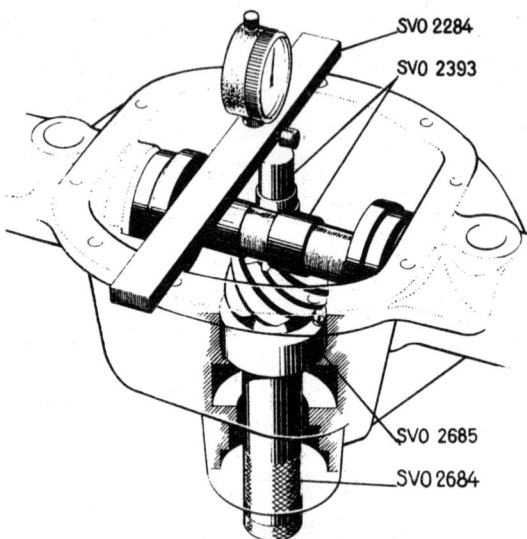

Fig. 82. — Setting up the tools for checking the pinion position. The dial indicator will be used to check the difference in position of the top of the gauge rod and the diameter of the tool SVO 2393.

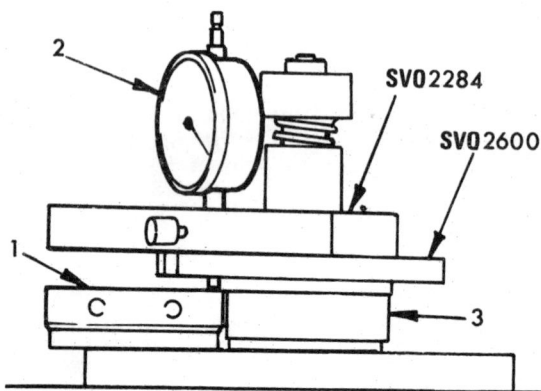

Fig. 83. — Determining the pinion bearing shim thickness with the special tools. The adjusting ring thickness (1) is to be compared with the bearing thickness (3) by means of the indicator (2).

83. Place the bearing to be used into the fixture after having "rubbed" it down into contact.

Zero the dial indicator to the adjuster ring thickness and then move the plunger to the bearing itself to show the actual thickness of shims required. Select suitable shims of the required thickness. The exact thickness will be difficult to obtain but the tolerance can be within 0.05 mm thinner but not more than 0.03 mm thicker than the measured dimension.

Press the pinion shaft rear bearing with sleeve SVO 2395.

NOTE: On a Volvo final drive the washer under the the rear bearing inner ring must NOT be fitted when re-conditioning.

Place in position the measured shims and press in both the outer bearing rings into the casing.

Insert the pinion into the casing and fit three 0.75 mm (0.03 in.) thick shims and the front pinion bearing. Fit tools SVO 2404 and 1845 and draw in the pinion shaft.

Pinion Bearing Pre-Load: Remove the tools from the pinion shaft and fit the flange and nut (but not the oil seal). Tighten the nut to 28 - 30 kgm (200 - 220 lb.ft.).

Refit the pinion gauge and dial indicator and measure the end float of the pinion head. Remove the pinion and take away shims corresponding to the clearance measured at the pinion head PLUS an additional 0.07 mm (0.003 in.).

Check the torque setting of the pinion shaft (values given in Section 7.1.) and re-adjust the shim thickness if necessary to obtain the required value.

Differential Installation: Crown wheel and pinion back-lash and differential bearing pre-load are both set by selection of the shims between the bearing inner tracks and the differential carrier in the following manner:

Lubricate the inside of the adjusting rings (SVO 2595) and fit them as shown in Fig. 84. Place the black-oxidised ring at the crown wheel side. Use a dial indicator to the crown wheel tooth flank and adjust the rings to

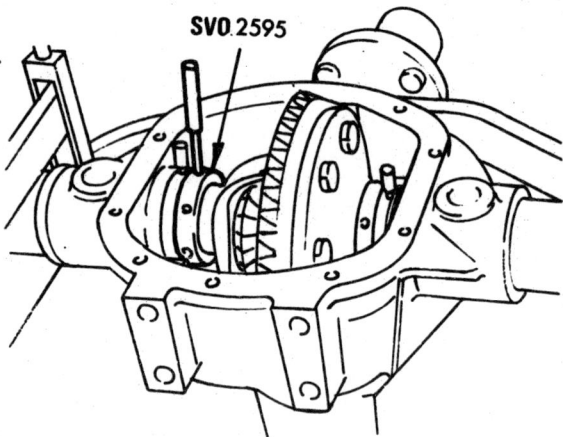

Fig. 84. — The adjuster rings (SVO 2595) in position on the differential carrier to set the crown wheel backlash and the carrier bearing pre-load. Once the adjusting rings have been set, their thickness is compared with the bearings in the same way as shown in Fig. 83.

obtain the correct gear flank clearance. Tighten the lock screws on the rings and check the tooth contact pattern.

Smear a little engineer's blue on the pinion teeth and transfer the marking to the crown wheel by holding the wheel and rotating the pinion back and forth. A correct tooth marking is shown in "A" in Fig. 85.

If the marking is not as required then the pinion position will need correction. Marking as in "B" will need to be corrected by moving the pinion inwards and marking as at "C" will require that the pinion is moved outwards. If the correct marking is not obtained then the pinion correction must be made before continuing the assembly.

Note that the contact pattern will tend to move a little towards the heel position once the actual bearings are fitted. When the correct backlash and contact pattern have been achieved remove the differential and adjusting rings from the casing.

Place the differential bearings in the measuring set-up (same as for the pinion bearing, already dealt with) and

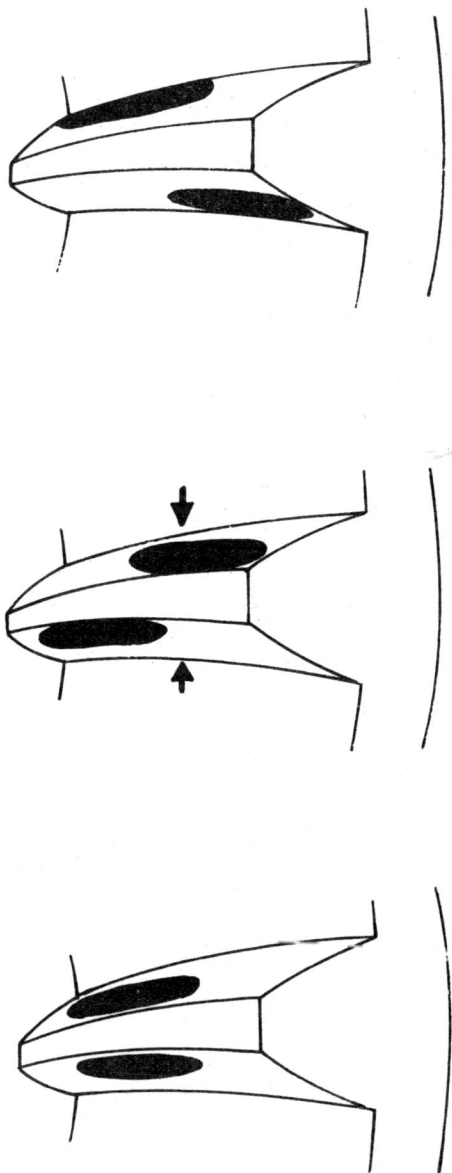

Fig. 85. — Crown wheel tooth markings. The correct marking is shown at "A". "B" and "C" show incorrect positioning of the drive pinion that must be corrected as described in Section 7.3.3.

133

measure the difference between the adjusting rings and the actual bearings to be used (take care not to mix up the two side adjusters and the bearings). Select a shim thickness that corresponds to the read-off value PLUS 0.07 mm (0.003 in.). Again take care that the two sides are not mixed up.

Fit the shims to the carrier and press on the bearings. Fit the expander tool as before (see Fig. 78) and tighten the bolt by 3 - 3 1/2 turns to allow the assembly to be fitted. Fit the caps and tighten the cap bolts to a torque of 5 - 7 kgm (36 - 50 lb.ft.).

Fit the pinion oil seal and the flange and nut. Complete the assembly of the cover and install the axle into the car.

7.5. Tightening Torque Values

Flange nut:	28 - 30 kgm (200 - 220 lb.ft.)
Differential carrier cap bolts:	5.0 - 7.0 kgm (35 - 50 lb.ft.)
Crown wheel bolts:	6.5 - 9.0 kgm (45 - 65 lb.ft.)
Wheel nuts:	10 - 14 kgm (70 - 100 lb.ft.)

8. BRAKES

8.0. Description

The Volvo 140 series vehicles are fitted with two separate independent braking systems. The foot brake system operates on all four wheels, with disc type brakes front and rear. The parking (handbrake) system is mechanically operated to both rear wheels and incorporates duo-servo drums mounted on the disc for the rear brakes.

The front disc brakes incorporate two pairs of cylinders that are completely independent of one another and are on separate hydraulic circuits from the tandem-type master cylinder. One of the circuits serves the lower cylinders of the front brakes and the right-hand rear wheel, while the other serves the upper cylinders of the front brakes and the left-hand rear wheel.

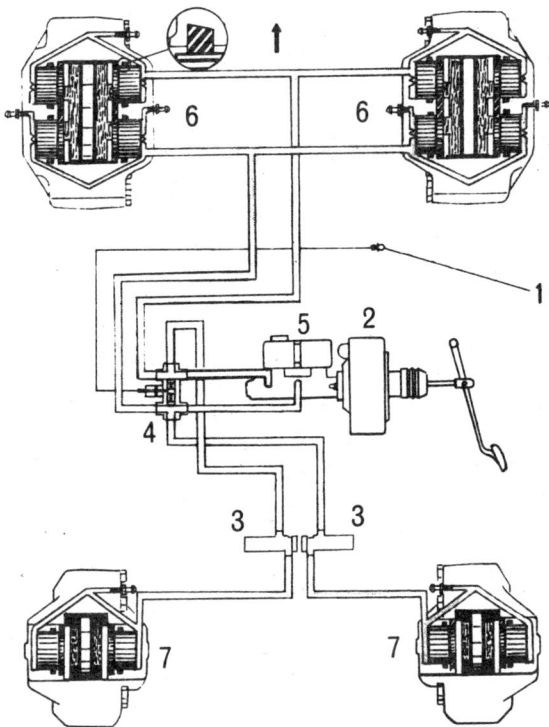

Fig. 86. — Diagram of the braking system.

1. Warning light
2. Servo unit
3. Proportioning valves
4. Brake warning valve
5. Master cylinder
   (tandem type)
6. Front disc brakes
7. Rear brakes

Vacuum servo-assistance is provided by a unit mounted between the pedal and the master cylinder.

Brake proportioning valves are fitted to both circuits and a warning valve provides a visual indication to the driver when there is an abnormal pressure difference between the two lines.

The disc brakes are self-adjusting and require no routine adjustment. The parking brakes are adjusted at the brake shoes or by adjustment of the cable.

Disc brake caliper units may be manufactured by Girling or ATE. Whilst the general construction of both types is similar the differences are outlined in the text where necessary. It should be noted that the Girling type brake is generally shown in the illustrations in this section.

8.1. Technical Data

FRONT DISC BRAKES

Type:	*Disc, four cylinders to each caliper*
Manufacturer:	*Girling or ATE*

Disc:

Outside diameter:	*272.2 mm (10.7 in.)*
Thickness:	
New — B20 E engine:	*14.28 - 14.4 mm (0.562 - 0.567 in.)*
— Other engines:	*12.7 - 12.8 mm (0.50 - 0.504 in.)*
Min. — B20 E engine:	*13.14 mm (0.557 in.)*
— Other B20 engines:	*11.6 mm (0.457 in.)*
Run-out:	*0.10 mm (0.004 in.)*

Pads:

Thickness, new:	*10 mm (0.394 in.)*
Effective area:	
Girling:	*150 sq.cm (23 sq.in.)*
ATE:	*140 sq.cm (22.5 sq.in.)*
Replace pad at thickness of:	*3 mm (0.125 in.)*
Minimum pad thickness:	*1.5 mm (0.062 in.)*

REAR DISC BRAKES

Type:	*Disc*

Disc:

Outside diameter:	*295.5 mm (11.63 in.)*
Thickness — New:	*9.6 mm (0.378 in.)*
— Minimum:	*8.4 mm (0.331 in.)*
Run-out (max.):	*0.15 mm (0.006 in.)*

Pads:

Thickness/pad replacement:	*As front*
Effective area:	
Girling:	*100 sq.cm (15.5 sq.in.)*
ATE:	*105 sq.cm (16.3 sq.in.)*

MASTER CYLINDER

Type:	Tandem
Nominal diameter:	22.2 mm (0.875 in.)
Cylinder bore (max.):	22.4 mm (0.882 in.)
Piston diameter (min.):	22.05 mm (0.868 in.)

BRAKE VALVE

Operating Pressure:	
142 and 144:	484 ± 28.4 psi
145:	711 ± 28.4 psi

SERVO-ASSISTANCE

Type:	Vacuum, direct operating
Make:	Girling
Type:	FD Type 50
Ratio:	1 : 3

PARKING BRAKE

Type:	Duo-servo drum
Operation:	Mechanical, rod and cable
Brake Drum:	
Diameter:	178.33 mm (7 in.) max.
Eccentricity, max.:	0.15 mm (0.006 in.)
Out-of-round, max.:	0.2 mm (0.008 in.)
Lining, effective area:	175 sq.cm (27 sq.in.)

BRAKE FLUID

Specification:	SAE J 1703
Also suitable:	DOT 3 or DOT 4

8.2.   Disc Brakes

8.2.0.   REPLACEMENT OF BRAKE PADS

The brake pads should be replaced when about 3 mm
(0.125 in.) of the lining remains. On no account should
the lining be allowed to reduce below the minimum of
1.5 mm (0.062 in.).

The components of a front brake unit are shown in Fig.
87. Details given in this section are applicable to both
front and rear brakes and the small differences between
Girling and ATE types are mentioned in the text.

Jack up the vehicle and support on stands as appropriate. Remove the road wheel.

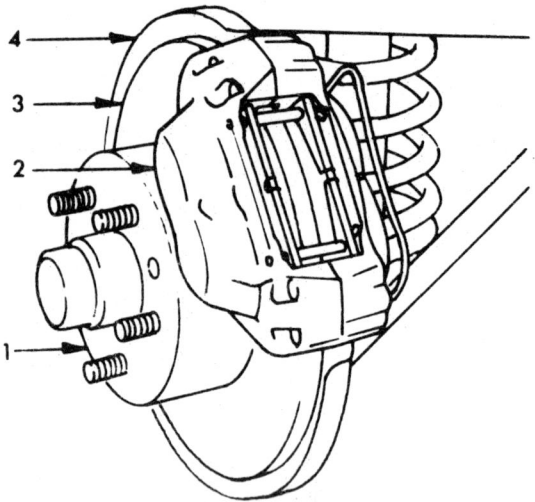

Fig. 87. — Front brake components.

1. Hub
2. Front caliper assembly
3. Brake disc
4. Back plate

Girling: Remove the hairpin shaped locking clips for the guide pins. Pull out one of the pins while holding the damper springs in place. Remove the springs and the other lock pin.

ATE: Tap out the upper guide pin, take out the tensioning spring and remove the lower pin. A 2.5 mm (9/64 in.) diameter punch will be necessary.

Pull out the pads, preferably with tool SVO 2917. If the used pads are to be refitted then mark them so that they are replaced in the same position.

Clean out the cavity into which the pads locate. Replace the dust covers if they are damaged. If dirt appears to have found its way past the cover then the brake unit should be serviced.

Press the pistons into the cylinders. This is best done with tool SVO 2809 but if done with another tool then great care must be taken not to damage or scratch the seal or pistons. Note that the fluid level in the reservoir will rise as the pistons are depressed and may spill if precautions are not taken.

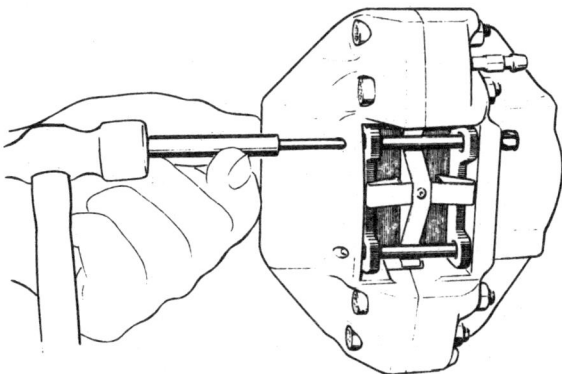

Fig. 88. — Removing the guide pin (ATE type brakes).

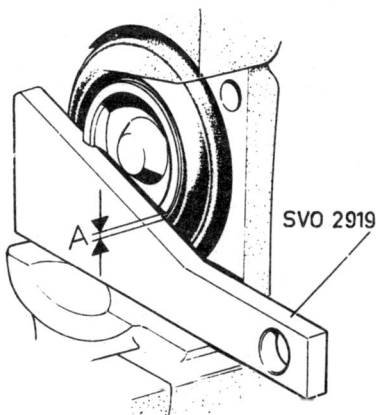

Fig. 89. — Checking the position of the pistons on the ATE type rear disc brakes.

ATE Rear Brakes: Check that the pistons are in the proper position to avoid brake squeal. Check with tool SVO 2919 as shown in Fig. 89. The piston recess should incline 20° and the dimension "A" should be a maximum of 1 mm (0.039 in.). Adjust, if necessary, by placing tool 2918 in position as in Fig. 90 and turn the piston as required.

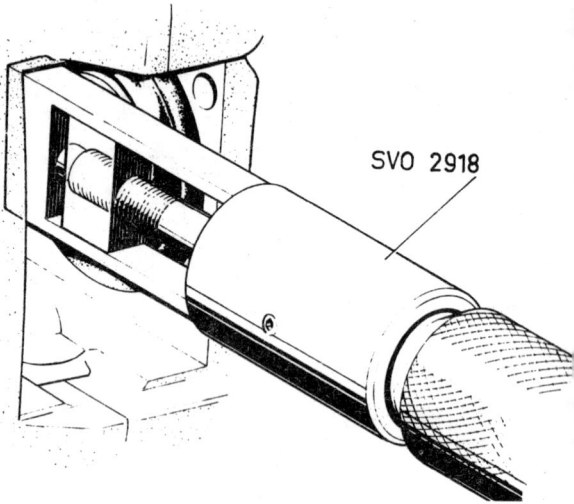

SVO 2918

Fig. 90. — Adjusting the piston on the ATE type rear disc brake.

Refit the pads as appropriate to the type. Fit new locking clips for the Girling type and new tensioning springs for ATE type.

Depress the brake pedal firmly several times to settle the new pads into position.

8.2.1. FRONT CALIPER UNITS — REMOVAL AND INSTALLATION

Refer to Figs. 91 and 92 for details of the front brake unit. Jack up and support the front of the car and off-load the control arms with a jack so that the brake hoses can be refitted without strain occurring when the suspension moves on the road.

Temporarily block the reservoir vent hole to prevent loss of fluid. Remove the road wheels. Remove the brake pipe clip and disconnect the hoses. Remove the two caliper attachment bolts and remove the unit. Block the pipe ends to prevent dirt entering the system.

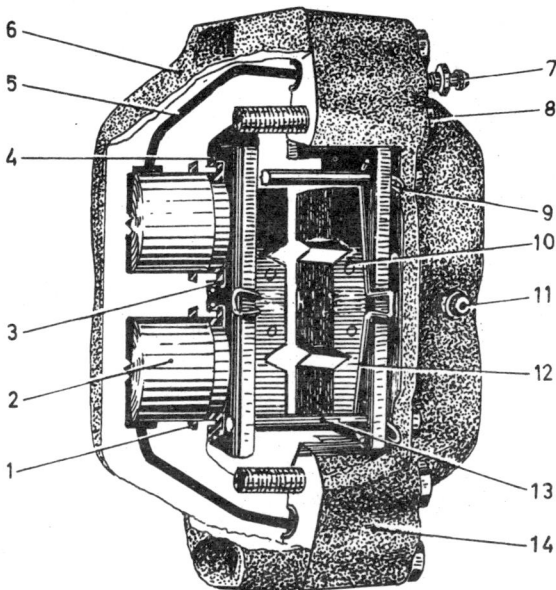

Fig. 91. — The front brake caliper assembly.

1.	Sealing ring
2.	Piston
3.	Dust cover
4.	Retainer ring
5.	Interconnection channel
6.)	Caliper, outer and
14.)	inner halves
7.	Upper bleeder nipple
8.	Caliper bolt
9.	Retaining clip
10.	Brake pad
11.	Lower bleeder nipple
12.	Damping spring clip
13.	Retainer pin

Install in the reverse sequence to removal, noting the following points:

Clean all contact surfaces before installation. Check the centring of the caliper to the disc. This should be the

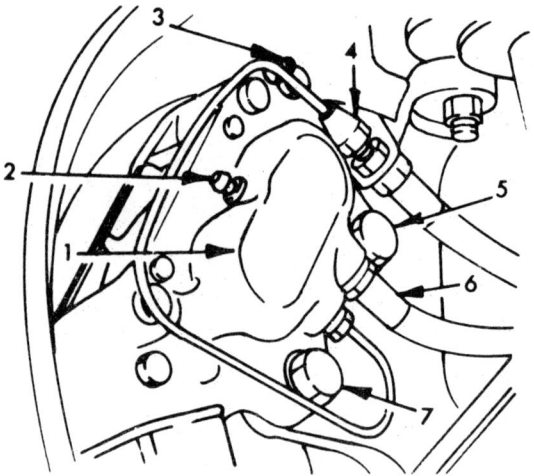

Fig. 92. — Front caliper and connections.

1. Caliper assembly
2. Lower bleeder nipple
3. Upper bleeder nipple
4. Connection for lower cylinder
5. Caliper attachment bolt
6. Connection for upper cylinder
7. Caliper attachment bolt

same on both sides within a maximum of 0.55 mm (0.02 in.). Shims in thicknesses of 0.2 and 0.4 mm (0.008 and 0.016 in.) are available.

Fit the caliper attachment bolts with two drops of Loctite AV to the threads. Refit the hoses, remove the reservoir vent hole plug and bleed the brake system.

IMPORTANT! The brake caliper halves, both front and rear, are NEVER to be separated.

8.2.2. REAR BRAKE CALIPER UNITS — REMOVAL AND INSTALLATION

The rear brake caliper unit is shown in Fig. 93. Removal and installation is carried out in a similar way to the front units, noting the following points:

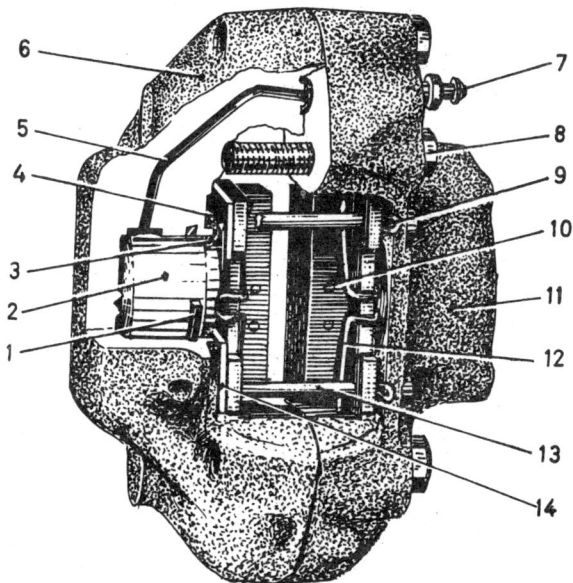

Fig. 93. — Rear brake caliper assembly.

1. Sealing ring
2. and piston
3. Dust cover and
4. retainer ring
5. Interconnection
   channel
6. Caliper, outer and
11. inner halves
7. Bleeder nipple
8. Caliper bolt
9. Retaining clip
10. Brake pad
12. Damping spring clip
13. Retainer pin
14. Washer

Centring of the caliper to the disc should be within 0.25 mm (0.010 in.) and caliper location shims are available in thicknesses of 0.60 - 1.8 mm (0.024 - 0.072 in.).

Chock the front wheels and release the handbrake when working on the rear brakes. Refit the hose and bleed the brakes.

8.2.3. BRAKE CALIPER UNITS – SERVICING

General instructions regarding work on the hydraulic units are given in the next section and these must be followed. Dismantle the caliper units by first removing the pads. Remove the retaining rings and the dust cover. Place a soft wood disc between the pistons and remove from the cylinders by using low pressure compressed air, applied to the brake pipe ports.

Remove the sealing rings and discard, make sure that the grooves are not damaged by any sharp edges on the tool that is used. Screw out the bleeder nipple and the brake line connectors.

Note the following points during assembly:

- Do not separate the two halves of the calipers.
- On the rear brake of ATE manufacture, make sure the pistons are in the proper position as already described.
- Coat all surfaces of the pistons and cylinders with brake fluid.

8.3. Servicing Notes – Brake System

Inspection and cleaning for the brake hydraulic system components follow a common procedure no matter which units are being dealt with. These points are, therefore, dealt with below and must be followed at all times.

Any of the components of the system must only be cleaned with brake fluid or denatured alcohol free from benzine. Methylated spirit is the only generally available fluid to this specification and this may be used as a cheaper alternative to brake fluid. If methylated spirit is used, do not allow the rubber parts to soak in the fluid for any length of time.

Petrol, white spirit or trichlorethylene must not be used for cleaning. Mineral oil and grease must never be allowed to come into contact with the system since they will all very rapidly destroy the rubber seals. Keep the hands clean and free from grease or dirt.

Inspect all parts carefully and reject any that show signs of wear or damage. Pay particular attention to any signs of corrosion or scoring of the cylinder bores and the pistons.

Replace all rubber seals each time the units are dismantled. Always obtain genuine manufacturer's spares and service kits.

Coat all parts in clean brake fluid before assembling; the alternative is the special rubber grease that can be obtained. Never assemble any part unless it has first been dried and thoroughly cleaned. Avoid the use of fluffy rags or cleaning tissue.

Never re-use fluid that has been drained from the system or that which has been used for cleaning or soaking parts. Remember that even the best quality brake fluid will gradually absorb water over a period of time and any servicing of the system will usually require that the complete system is drained and refilled with new fluid.

The cost of a new set of seals or a system refill is a small price to pay for safe motoring and we recommend that no doubtful component is ever refitted into the system.

8.4.   Master Cylinder

8.4.0.   REMOVAL AND INSTALLATION

Remove the master cylinder by referring to Fig. 94. Take off the connections for the pipes and fit plastic plugs to prevent dirt entering the system. Remove the two attachment nuts and lift the cylinder assembly forwards to remove.

CAUTION!   Do not depress the brake pedal with the cylinder removed.

When installing the master cylinder, the clearance between the primary piston and the servo thrust rod must be set as shown in Fig. 95. The clearance is shown at "C" and is set by adjustment of the servo rod screw head so that the clearance is 0.1 - 1.0 mm (0.004 - 0.04 in.).

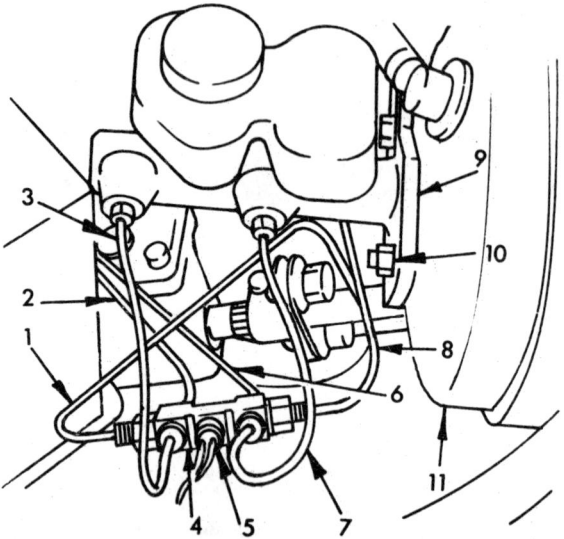

Fig. 94. — The master cylinder, servo and warning valve.

1. To left brake valve
2. To six-way union, lower
3. From secondary circuit,
   master cylinder
4. Warning valve
5. Warning switch
6. To six-way union, upper
7. From primary circuit,
   master cylinder
8. To right brake valve
9. Master cylinder
10. Attachment nut
11. Servo unit

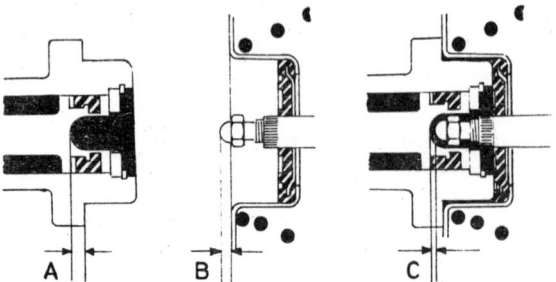

Fig. 95. — Adjusting the servo unit thrust rod for the correct
clearance (C) to the master cylinder piston (refer to Section
8.4.0.).

146

Measure the two dimensions "A" and "B" and set to the value given. The dimension "B" is set when the thrust rod is fully in, with the engine running to provide the necessary vacuum. When adjusting the servo thrust rod apply two drops of Loctite type B to the threads.

Fit the master cylinder and tighten the nuts to 2.4 kgm (17 lb.ft.). Refill the system and bleed.

8.4.1. MASTER CYLINDER — SERVICING

Fix the master cylinder in a vice fitted with soft jaws and pull up the reservoir with both hands to remove it from the body. Remove the rubber seals from the cylinder.

Refer to Fig. 96 and dismantle the parts after removing the stop screw. Note the position and disposition of each part as it is removed. Remove the seals, taking care not to damage or scratch the pistons.

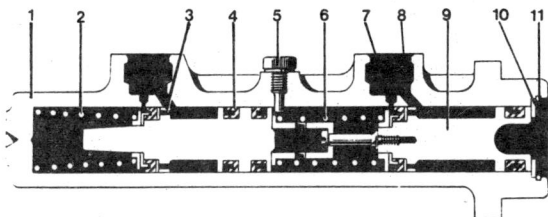

Fig. 96. — Section through the master cylinder.

1. Cylinder body
2. Return spring, secondary piston
3. Secondary piston
4. Piston seal
5. Stop screw
6. Return spring, primary piston
7. Equalising hole
8. Overflow hole
9. Primary piston
10. Washer
11. Circlip

Clean and examine all parts. Follow the general instructions given in Section 8.3. Measure the cylinder bore and the pistons and compare to the values given in the "Technical Data".

In addition to the piston seals the stop screw, washer and lock ring should be replaced with new parts; also the rubber seals for the reservoir.

Fit the new seals to the secondary piston as shown in Fig. 97. Seals (7 and 8) should be fitted with tool SVO 5004. If not available make up a "bullet-nosed" adaptor to allow the seal to be slid on over the sharp edge of the piston.

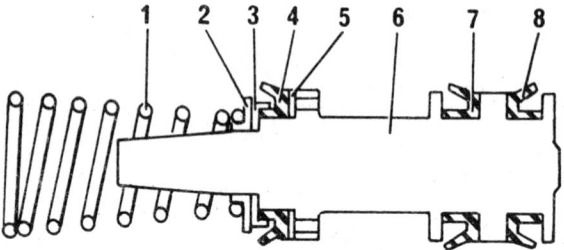

Fig. 97. — Secondary piston of the master cylinder.

1. } 2. }	Spring and spring plate
3.	Back-up ring
4.	Piston seal
5.	Washer
6.	Piston
7. } 8. }	Piston seals

Assemble the new primary piston as shown in Fig. 98. Coat the pistons with brake fluid and assemble into the cylinder in their proper order. Fit the washer and circlip. Fit the stop screw and washer; tighten to 1 - 1.2 kgm (7 - 9 lb.ft.).

Check that the equalising hole is clean (7, Fig. 96). If the pistons have been correctly assembled the hole will be clear of the piston and seal (use a soft wire of 0.5 mm diameter to check).

Fit the rubber seals and the reservoir parts. Check that the vent hole is clean and not blocked.

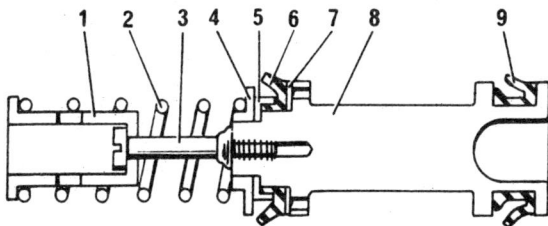

Fig. 98. — Primary piston of the master cylinder.

1. Sleeve
2. Spring
3. Screw
4. Thrust washer
5. Back-up ring
6. Piston seal
7. Washer
8.)
9.) Piston and piston seal

8.5. Brake Proportioning Valves

The brake valves cannot be repaired and must be changed if faulty. Checking of the valves should be carried out by a dealer or distributor.

8.6. Bleeding the Brake System

Bleeding of the system should be carried out in the order shown in Fig. 99. Note the three bleed points on each front wheel caliper.

Depress the brake pedal several times to remove any residual vacuum from the servo unit. Clean around the reservoir cap and fill the container to the "Max." mark. Remove the brake warning switch.

Attach a plastic tube to the first bleed point and dip the free end into a clean container about a quarter full of brake fluid. Make sure that the end of the tube is always below the surface of the fluid. Use a 5/16 in. ring spanner to open the bleed screw by half a turn and have an assistant ready to depress the brake pedal. Slowly press the pedal downwards to a full stroke. Pause a second or so and then allow the pedal to return quickly.

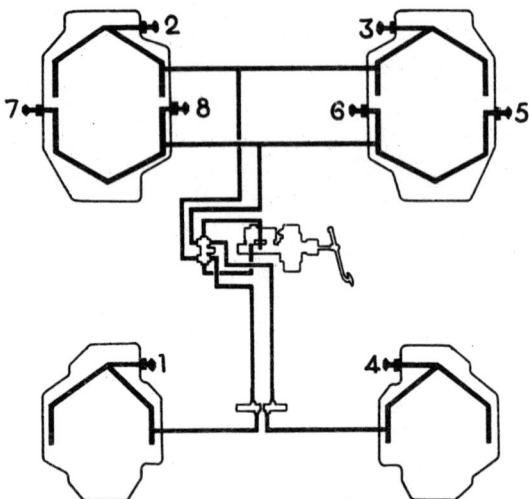

Fig. 99. — The sequence for bleeding the hydraulic system.

1. Left rear wheel
2. Left front wheel, upper/inner
3. Right front wheel, upper/inner
4. Right rear wheel
5. Right front, outer
6. Right front, lower/inner
7. Left front, outer
8. Left front, lower/inner

Repeat the sequence until no more air bubbles appear in the fluid container. Close the bleeder screw when the brake pedal is held fully depressed. Top up the fluid in the reservoir as necessary and proceed to the remaining bleed points.

Fit the warning switch and tighten to a torque of 1.4 - 2 kgm (10 - 15 lb.ft.).

8.7. Brake Pedal

The brake pedal should travel 140 mm (5.5 in.) at full stroke and at the bottom position the pedal should be about 10 mm (0.375 in.) from the floor. Obviously, these dimensions can only be checked with the hydraulic circuits disconnected (alternatively with both circuits open for bleeding). Remember that the pedal must not be depressed without the master cylinder in position.

Adjust the pedal position, if necessary, by removing the split pin from the clevis and adjusting the length of the rod.

Adjust the brake light switch so that, with the pedal in the free position, the distance between the pedal edge and the threaded brass sleeve on the switch is 4 ± 2 mm $(0.16 \pm 0.08$ in.).

8.8.   Brake Servo Unit

8.8.0.   REMOVAL AND INSTALLATION

Remove the master cylinder and then remove the split pin and pin from the pedal clevis. Remove the vacuum hose from the check valve and take out the attachment bolts for the brackets to allow the servo to be removed.

Install in the reverse sequence. Note that if the clevis has been removed from the rod, the correct initial setting is with a dimension of about 45 mm (1.8 in.) between the clevis pin bore centre line and the locking surface of the rock locknut.

8.8.1.   SERVICING

The servo unit is shown in Fig. 100, but it is not recommended that servicing should be attempted. Note that failure of the unit will have no effect on the braking efficiency of the vehicle other than to require a heavier pressure on the pedal for the same retardation.

The check valve can be removed quite easily with two screwdrivers since it is held in only by ridges engaging in the sealing ring. Fit a new valve and seal ring and carefully press in the valve after having smeared the special grease (supplied in the repair kit) onto the seal.

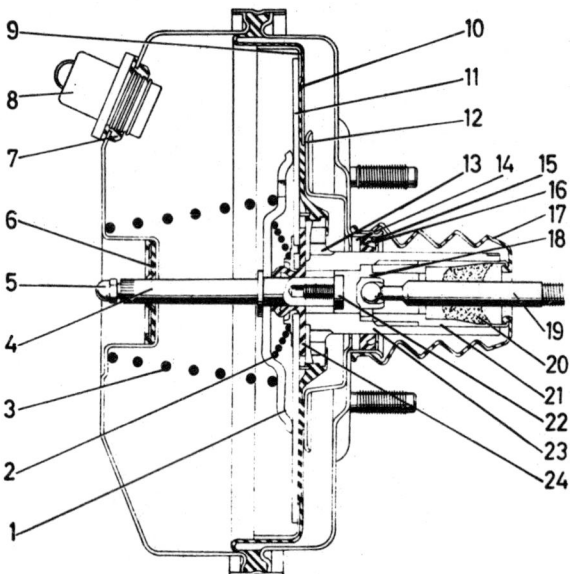

Fig. 100. — The vacuum servo unit in a sectional view.

1.	Thrust washer
2.	Valve spring
3.	Return spring
4.	Thrust rod, to master cylinder
5.	Adjusting screw
6.	Seal ring
7. 8.	Seal and check valve
9. 10.	Guide and diaphragm
11.	Piston discs
12.	Rear flange
13.	Relief valve
14.	Guide
15.	Seal ring
16.	Lock washer
17.	Rubber boot
18.	Air inlet
19.	Thrust rod, from pedal
20.	Filter
21.	Plastic sleeve
22.	Bolt
23. 24.	Valve housing and plate

Fit a new air filter by easing off the rubber cover and withdrawing the filter. The new part must be slid over the push rod after removal of the clevis and nut.

8.9.   Handbrake

8.9.0.   ADJUSTMENT

The handbrake should be fully on at the third or fourth notch. If it is not, the adjustment is made first at the brake drum and then at the pull rod at the centre of the car. Both these points can be seen in Fig. 101.

To make the adjustment of the shoes, chock the front wheels and jack up and support the rear of the car. Take off the wheels and release the handbrake lever.

Check that the brake pads are not stuck to the brake disc. To prevent the shoes of the handbrake rubbing while the adjustment is being carried out. Tool 2742 should be applied to the spring as shown in Fig. 102. If this tool is not available then release the cable from the lever.

Set the hole in the brake drum at the 12 o'clock position and insert a screwdriver to engage with the adjuster teeth. Move the screwdriver blade upwards to tighten the shoes. When the drum is locked, turn the adjuster back by 4 - 5 serrations. Check that the drum does not "drag" by rotating in the normal direction of travel. Very little drag is permitted so release the adjuster by a further 2 - 3 serrations if necessary.

Repeat for the other wheel and then remove the tool from the spring. Apply the handbrake and check that it is full on at the 3rd/4th notch. If not, the cable should be tensioned. Tension the cable by adjustment of the pull rod (5, Fig. 101).

8.9.1.   REPLACING THE CABLE

With the rear of the car jacked up and supported, and the handbrake lever released, take off the pulley from the block.

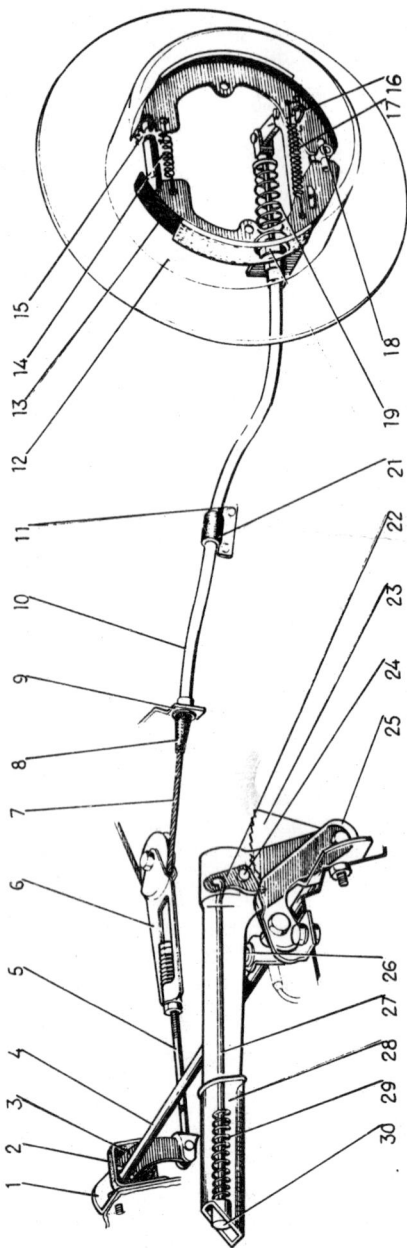

Fig. 101. — Handbrake mechanism (parking brake).

1.)
2.) Support attachment,
3.) rubber cover and lever
4. Shaft
5. Pull rod
6. Block, equaliser
7. Cable

8.) Rubber boot and
9.) front attachment
10. Cable sleeve
11. Attachment
12. Brake drum
13. Secondary shoe
14. Return spring

15. Adjuster
16. Lever
17. Moveable rod
18. Anchor bolt
19. Return spring
20. Rear attachment
21. Rubber cable guide

22. Pawl
23. Ratchet
24. Rivet
25. Outside support attachment
26. Warning switch
27. Push rod
28. Handbrake lever
29.) Spring and push
30.) button

Remove the rubber cover and nut from the front attachments. Place tool 2742 in position as before (Fig. 102) and remove the pivot pin so that the cable can be released from the lever. Remove the spring, washer and nut and lift the cable out.

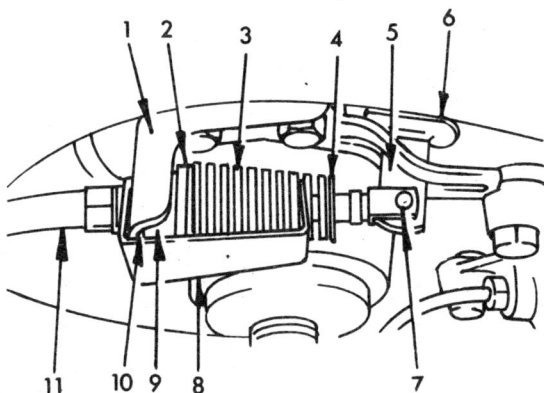

Fig. 102. — Installing the clamp tool to the handbrake cable return spring.

1.	Cable attachment
2.	Washer
3.	Return spring
4.	Washer
5.	Lever
6.	Rubber cover
7.	Lever pin
8.	Tool SVO 2742
9.	Nut
10.	Lock washer
11.	Cable sleeve

Install in the reverse sequence. Fit new rubber cable guides for the cable suspension. Grease the pivot pins and other parts.

8.9.2.   FITTING NEW BRAKE SHOES

If the brake shoes or linings are to be replaced, note the following points:

First slacken the locknut to remove tension from the cable. Note the position of each part as it is dismantled and be sure to replace in the same way. The primary and secondary shoes are placed as shown in Fig. 103.

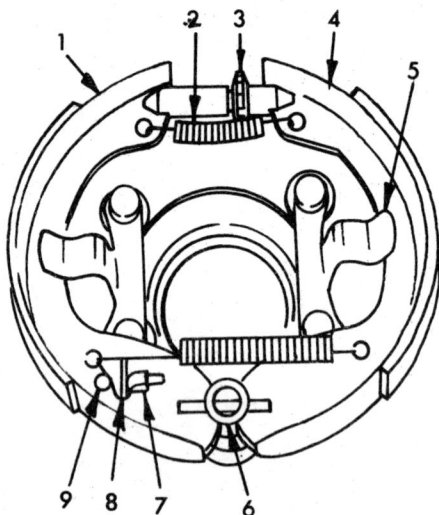

Fig. 103. — Parking brake assembly.

1.) Primary shoe and upper
2.) return spring
3. Adjuster
4. Secondary shoe
5. Shoe retainer
6. Anchor bolt
7. Lever
8.) Washer and spring
9.)

Apply a little high-melting point grease to the backing plate where it contacts the shoes, also to the lever and adjusting screw. Hook on the return spring ends from the front of the shoes.

Check the internal surface of the drum. Polish off any rust spots and check that it is not out-of-round by more than 0.2 mm (0.008 in.). Adjust the brake shoes and the cable as already described.

8.10.   Tightening Torque Values

Wheel nuts: 10 - 14 kgm (70 - 100 lb.ft.)
Caliper attachment bolts:

Front:	9.0 - 10 kgm (65 - 70 lb.ft.)
Rear:	6.0 - 7.0 kgm (45 - 50 lb.ft.)
Stop screw, master cylinder:	1.0 - 1.2 kgm (7 - 9 lb.ft.)
Attachment nuts, master	
cylinder:	2.4 kgm (17 lb.ft.)
Bleeder nipples:	0.4 - 0.6 kgm (3 - 4.5 lb.ft.)
Brake hose, front caliper:	1.6 - 2.0 kgm (12 - 15 lb.ft.)
Warning valve switch:	1.4 - 2.0 kgm (10 - 15 lb.ft.)
Brake pipes:	1.1 - 1.5 kgm (8 - 11 lb.ft.)
Plug, brake valve:	10 - 12 kgm (70 - 85 lb.ft.)
Locknut, brake valve:	2.5 - 3.5 kgm (18 - 25 lb.ft.)

9.   WHEELS AND TYRES

9.0.   Wheels — Technical Data

Type:	Disc
Designation:	
142, 144 De-Luxe and	
Grand Luxe:	5 J x 15 L
145 De-Luxe:	5 J x 15 H
142 and 144:	4.5 J x 15 L
145 and 145 Express:	4.5 J x 15 H
Radial throw (max.):	1.6 mm (0.063 in.)
Warp (max.):	1.6 mm (0.063 in.)
Inbalance, complete wheel:	7.8 lb.in.
Wheel tightening torque (nuts):	10 - 14 kgm (72 - 101 lb.ft.)

9.1.   Tyres — Technical Data

Type:	Tubeless
Size:	
142 and 144:	165 SR 15-4 PR
145:	165 S 15-8-PR. 165 SR 15-4-PR
U.S.A.:	6.85 S 15-8-PR

Tyre Pressures (cold, normal load):

Model 142, 144: 165R15:

Front:	1.8 kg/sq.cm (26 psi)
Rear:	1.9 kg/sq.cm (27 psi)
Maximum:	2.5 kg/sq.cm (36 psi)

Model 142, 144: C78-15 (4PR):

Front:	1.5 kg/sq.cm (21 psi)
Rear:	1.6 kg/sq.cm (23 psi)
Maximum:	2.3 kg/sq.cm (32 psi)

Model 145: 175R15:

Front:	1.7 kg/sq.cm (25 psi)
Rear:	1.8 kg/sq.cm (26 psi)
Maximum:	2.8 kg/sq.cm (40 psi)

Model 145: C78-15 (8PR):
    Front: *1.5 kg/sq.cm (21 psi)*
    Rear: *1.8 kg/sq.cm (26 psi)*
    Maximum: *2.8 kg/sq.cm (40 psi)*

NOTE: For sustained high speed driving over 120 kph (75 mph) increase the cold pressures by 0.28 kg/sq.cm (4 psi) but DO NOT exceed the maximum values given in brackets above.

10.   EXHAUST EMISSION CONTROL

10.0.   Introduction

Various systems of exhaust emission control are fitted to the Volvo 140 series of vehicles dependent on the market for which the car is intended. The early engines do not include such features but the current range of B20 engines are all fitted with one or other of the systems detailed below.

The positive crankcase ventilation system is a relatively simple arrangement which involves no changes to the fuel system. The remaining systems are, however, more complicated and it is not recommended that the owner should carry out more than the routine maintenance outlined. Both fuel and ignition systems must be kept in good order and be properly adjusted for these latter systems to operate properly. Special equipment and tools are necessary to check and adjust the systems and it is recommended that a dealer or distributor carry out all such work.

10.1.   Positive Crankcase Ventilation

The system is shown in Fig. 104. At intervals of 40,000 km (24,000 miles) clean the nipple (3) and flame guard.

For U.S.A. vehicles this work should be carried out at the 20,000 km (12,000 miles) servicing. Check the hoses at the same time and replace any that are in poor condition.

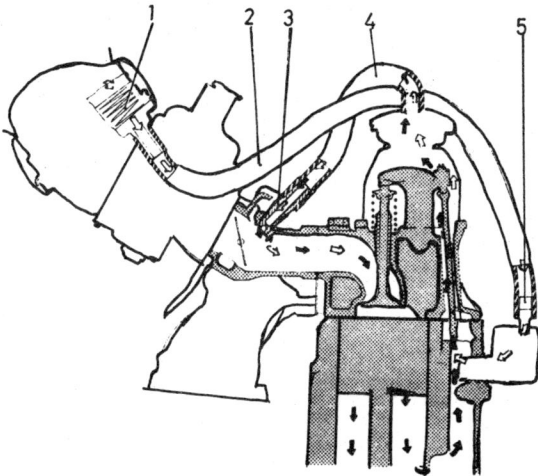

Fig. 104. — Positive crankcase ventilation system.

1.   Cleaner insert
2.   Hose for fresh air supply
3.   Nipple
4.   Hose for crankcase gases
5.   Flame guard

10.2.   Exhaust Gas Re-Circulation

The system consists of an EGR valve coupled by hoses to the exhaust manifold and the intake manifold, with a control hose for the vacuum operated valve connected to the carburettor venturi.

Synchronisation of the carburettors is particularly important to ensure the proper functioning of the system.

The EGR valve and hose lines should be cleaned at intervals of 20,000 km (12,000 miles). Every 40,000 km (24,000 miles), that is, at every other cleaning, the EGR valve should be replaced with a new one.

10.3.   Gas Evaporative Control System

The components of this system are as below and the changes to the carburettor are also described:

The fuel tank is sealed by the filler cap and an expansion tank is fitted to lead fuel fumes to a venting filter in the engine compartment. Fuel fumes from the carburettor float chamber are led to the venting valve via a hot start valve that is only open when the engine has been switched off or is idling.

An air valve, at the top of the venting filter, controls the connection between the venting filter and the carburettor venturi.

It should be noted that the hot start valve is to be found on all current vehicles with twin carburettors. In this case there is, however, no hose connected to the valve outlet and the fumes are vented to atmosphere.

10.4.   Air Cleaner — Constant Air Temperature Unit

The constant air temperature unit is identified by the two flexible hoses, one of which is attached to the exhaust pipe. A thermostat fitted to the unit opens and closes a flap valve so that the proportions of cold and hot air are always at around 90° F when they reach the carburettor intake.

11.   AIR CONDITIONING

11.0.   Servicing Notes

The Volvo series 140 vehicles may be fitted with an optional air conditioning unit which is shown in Fig. 105.

The system operates as a compressor type in which the refrigerant is circulated by a compressor driven from the engine. We do not recommend, under any circumstances, that the owner should undertake any dismantling of the sealed pressurised system.

If a major overhaul of the engine is to be carried out it is recommended that the vehicle is taken to a dealer or specialist for the system to be de-pressurised before commencing work and then again for re-pressurisation and reconnection at the completion of the servicing.

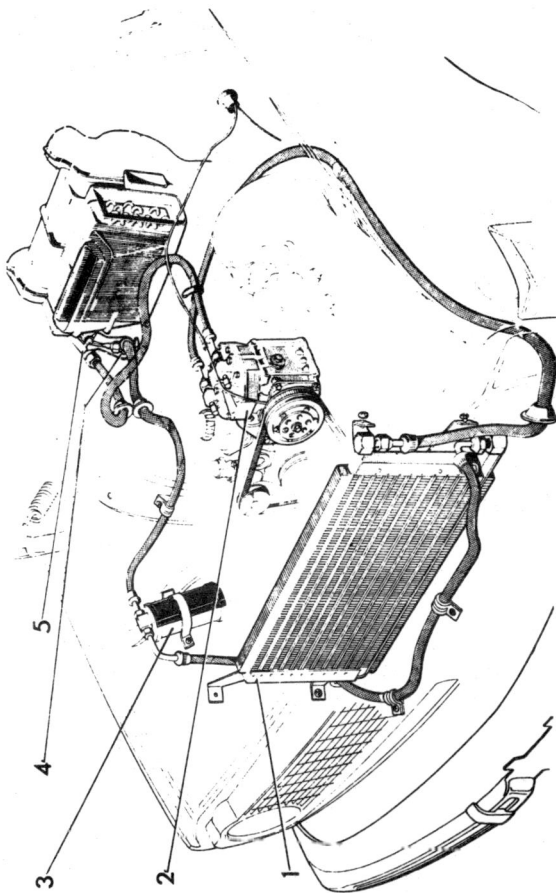

Fig. 105. — The air conditioning system as fitted to the Volvo 140 series vehicles.

1. Condenser
2. Compressor
3. Dryer
4. Expansion valve
5. Evaporator

If these precautions are carried out there is no reason why normal servicing of the engine or any other parts should not be carried out since it is quite simple to remove the various units once the system has been de-pressurised. Take care that all units are properly protected to avoid the possibility of dirt or foreign matter finding its way into the pressure system.

12. - ELECTRICAL EQUIPMENT

12.0. Battery

Type:	
Early models:	Boliden 107 GM 60 or equivalent
Current models:	Tudor 6 EX 3 op, or equivalent

System voltage:	12 volts
Earth (ground):	Negative terminal
Standard capacity:	60 A/h

Specific Gravity:	
Fully charged:	1.28
Needing re-charge:	1.21

12.1. Generator (Dynamo)

12.1.0. INTRODUCTION

A D.C. dynamo is fitted to early model vehicles, together with a control box and details are given in the following sections. It is not recommended that the control box should be adjusted by the owner.

12.1.1. REMOVAL AND INSTALLATION

Remove the dynamo by disconnecting the negative battery terminal and then remove the dynamo cables from the terminals. Loosen the tensioning bracket bolt and take off the vee belt. Remove the mounting bolts and take off the dynamo.

Install in the reverse sequence and tension the belt to the proper value.

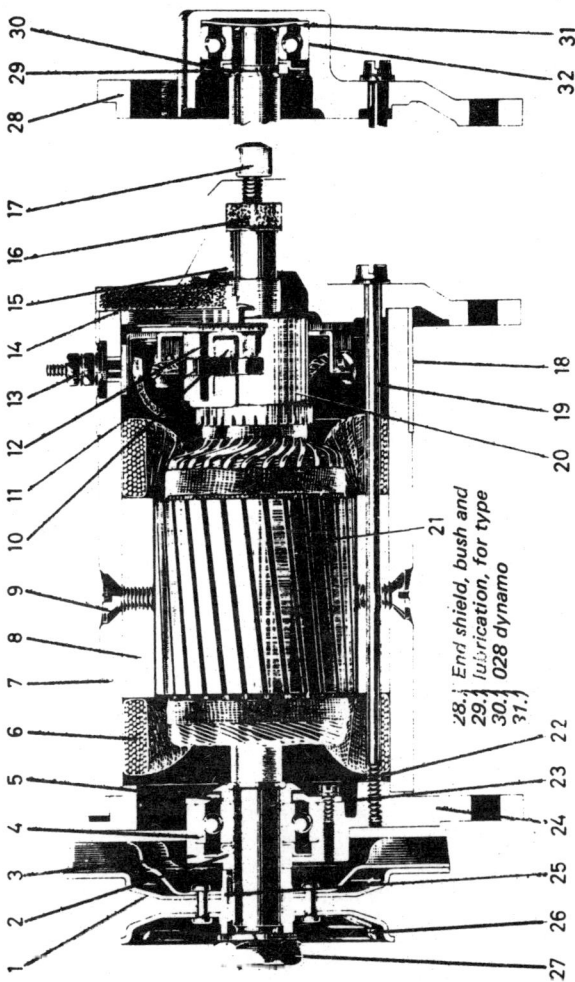

Fig. 106. — Section through the dynamo fitted to early vehicles.

1. Pulley
2.) Spacer ring and oil
3.) seal washer
4.) Ball bearing and
5.) spacer
6. Field winding
7. Stator
8.)
9.) Pole shoe and screw
10.)
11.) Brush holder and spring
12. Brush
13. Terminal
14.) End shield, bush and
15.) lubrication, for type
16.) 036 dynamo
17.) 028 dynamo
18.) Protective band
19.) and screw
20. Commutator
21. Armature
22.) Screw and seal washer
23.)
24. End shield
25.) Key and spring washer
26.)
27. Nut

28.) End shield, bush and
29.) lubrication, for type
30.) 028 dynamo
31.)

163

12.1.2. SERVICING AND CHECKING

The dynamo is shown in Fig. 106. If the dynamo does not charge properly the fault will be either in the dynamo itself, in the control box or in some open circuit condition in the cables. Obviously, the first check will be with the drive belt for condition and proper tension. If these are correct then carry out the following tests with the dynamo still in the vehicle:

Connect a voltmeter negative lead to the chassis or a good earth connection, and the other terminal to the "B1" terminal of the control relay. The indicated voltage, with the dynamo rotating fairly fast, should not be less than the battery voltage. An erratic reading will point to some fault in leads or terminal connections. A zero reading indicates an open circuit.

Disconnect the dynamo leads and join terminal "DF" to "D1". Connect the voltmeter between the two terminals and the yoke and start the engine. The voltage should rise steadily as the speed of the engine is raised to around 2,000 rpm.

Remove the cover band and inspect the brushes for wear. Also inspect for any sluggish movement of the brushes and rectify if necessary.

Unscrew the through bolts and inspect the commutator. Clean with a petrol-moistened cloth. If necessary, clean with fine grade glass paper (never use emery cloth). If in poor condition the commutator can be skimmed in a high-speed lathe. Undercut the insulators with a ground-down hacksaw blade and undercut to a depth of 0.8 - 1 mm (0.032 - 0.040 in.).

Check the field coils and armature windings for open circuit and short circuit to earth.

12.1.3. TECHNICAL DATA — DYNAMO

Type:
B18 A:	*Bosch LJ/GG 240/12/2400 AR 6*
B18 B:	*Bosch LJ/GG 240/12/2400 AR 7*
Ground (earth):	*Negative terminal*

Brushes:
Type: WSK 43L-1
Number: 2
Contact pressure: 450 - 600 g (1 - 1.3 lb.)

Field winding resistance: 4.8 +0.5 ohms
Commutator insulation
  undercut: 0.8 - 1.0 mm
                  (0.032 - 0.040 in.)
Max. continuous current: 30 amps

12.1.4. TECHNICAL DATA – DYNAMO CONTROL BOX

Type:	Bosch RS/VA 240/12/12
Equalising resistance aR:	15.5 - 16.5 ohms
Control resistance wR:	8 - 9 ohms

Test Values:
  Reverse current relay:
    Adjusted to cut in at: 12.4 - 13.1 volts
    Adjusted for reverse
      current at: 2.0 - 7.5 amps
  Voltage control:
    Control voltage:
      No-load: 14.1 - 14.8 volts
      On-load: 13.0 - 14.0 volts
  Charging current:
    Cold dynamo at voltage
      control: 45 amps
    Warm dynamo at
      voltage control: 30 amps

12.2. Alternator

12.2.0. SERVICE NOTES AND PRECAUTIONS

The following special instructions must always be observed on vehicles fitted with an alternator:

— Always make sure that the battery is connected with the correct polarity. Incorrect polarity will, even if only for an instant, cause immediate damage to the alternator diodes.

— Never disconnect the battery, alternator or control box leads with the engine running.

— Before charging a battery while installed in the vehicle, remove the negative cable.

— Do not use a rapid charger as an aid to starting.

— The battery voltage is always impressed on the alternator while the leads are connected. Take great care not to short out the terminals with a metal tool (the battery should always be disconnected while working on the vehicle). Do not spray the alternator with water or any other fluid.

— Disconnect the battery and alternator leads BEFORE using any form of electric welding equipment on the car.

Testing and servicing of the alternator and control box is best left to a specialist. Incorrect application of test instruments can result in damage and failure of the units.

It should be noted that there are two different alternators and control boxes. On no account should a different type of alternator or control box be fitted.

They will not be compatable and damage will result.

12.2.1. TECHNICAL DATA — ALTERNATORS

Type S.E.V. Marshall A-14/30 (7120202)

Output:	490 watts
Max. amperage:	35 amps
Min. brush length:	5 mm (0.2 in.)
Tightening Torque:	
Attachment screws:	0.28 - 0.3 kgm (2 - 2.2 lb.ft.)
Pulley nut:	4 kgm (29 lb.ft.)
Test Values:	
Field winding resistance:	5.2 ± 0.2 ohms
Output test:	30 amps at 3,000 rpm and 13 volts

Type S.E.V. Marshall 14 V-34833 (14V 55A):

Output:	770 watts
Max. amperage:	55 amps
Min. brush length:	5 mm (0.2 in.)
Tightening torque values:	
Attachment screws:	0.28 - 0.3 kgm (2 - 2.2 lb.ft.)
Pulley nut:	4 kgm (29 lb.ft.)
Test Values:	
Field winding resistance:	3.7 ohms
Output test:	48 amps at 3,000 rpm and approx. 14 volts

Type Bosch KI-14V 35A 20:

Output:	*490 watts*
Max. amperage:	*35 amps*
Min. diameter of slip rings:	*31.5 mm (1.24 in.)*
Min. brush length:	*8 mm (0.31 in.)*
Brush pressure:	*6.6 - 8.8 lb.*
Pulley tightening torque:	*3.5 - 4 kgm (25 - 29 lb.ft.)*

Test Values:
Resistance — Stator:	*0.26 +0.03 ohms*
— Rotor:	*4.0 +0.4 ohms*
Output test:	*35 amps at 6,000 rpm and 14 volts*

12.2.2. TECHNICAL DATA — CONTROL BOXES

Type S.E.V. Motorola 14V 33525:
Control voltage (cold):	*13.1 - 14.4 volts*

Type S.E.V. Motorola 14V 33544:
Control voltage (cold):	*13.1 - 14.4 volts*

Type Bosch AD-14V:
Control voltage at 4,000 rpm (alternator) and cold regulator:	*14 - 15 volts*
Load current, lower contacts:	*28 - 30 amps*
Control range between upper and lower contacts:	*0 - 0.3 volt*
Load current, upper contacts:	*3 - 8 amps*

12.2.3. REMOVAL AND INSTALLATION

Disconnect the negative battery cable and disconnect the leads at the alternator. Loosen the bolt for the adjustment arm and remove the fan belt. Remove the attachment bolt and lift off the alternator.

Install in the reverse sequence to removal and adjust the belt tension. It is most important that any adjustment leverage is only applied at the front end of the alternator and NEVER at the rear end.

12.2.4. SERVICING

A typical alternator (S.E.V. Marshall) is shown in an exploded view in Fig. 107. The rotor bearings are sealed

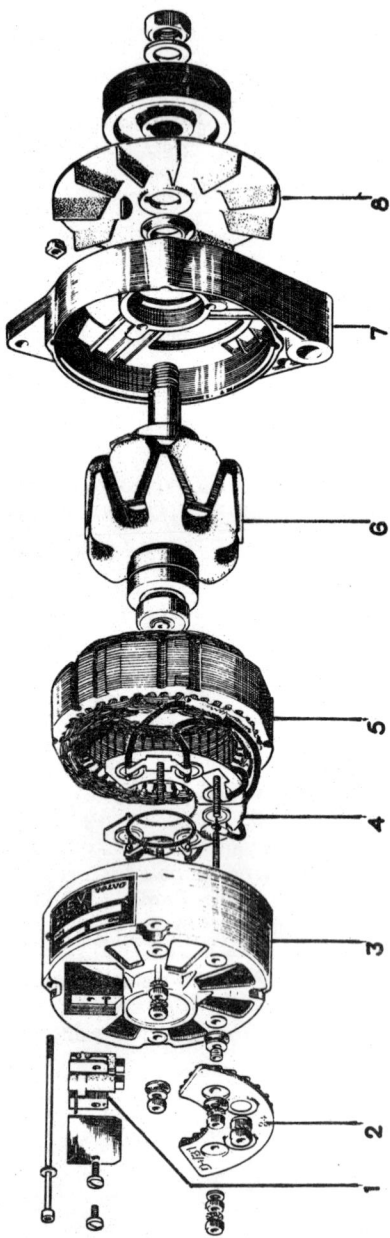

Fig. 107. — Exploded view of typical alternator (S.E.V. Marshall 14V-348331).

1. Brush holder
2. Diodes with holder
3. Slip ring end shield
4. Silicone diode rectifiers

5. Stator and rotor
6.
7. Drive end shield
8. and fan

168

and pre-lubricated and require no routine attention. The brush gear is accessible from the end cover. Since the brushes operate onto plain slip rings their life can be expected to be very much better than with a conventional dynamo, using a segmented commutator. If the slip rings are dirty, clean them with a little trichrorethene on a cloth. Polish with a fine grade of sand paper only if necessary (never use emery cloth).

12.3.   Fan Belt Tension

The fan belt tension should be such that the belt can be deflected by 10 mm (approx. 3/8 in.) by a force applied midway between the water pump pulley and the alternator (or dynamo). The force necessary to produce this deflection should be in accordance with the following values:

Vehicle with LHD:	*7 - 10 kg (15.5 - 22 lb.)*
Vehicle with RHD:	*5.5 - 7 kg (12 - 15.5 lb.)*
Vehicle with RHD and air conditioning:	*8.5 - 10 kg (19 - 22 lb.)*

12.4.   Starter Motor

12.4.0.   TECHNICAL DATA

Type:	*Bosch GF 12 V 1 PS*
Rotation:	*Clockwise*
Output:	*Approx. 736 W (I hp)*
Number of brushes:	*4*
Solenoid, cut-in voltage:	*Min. 8 volts*
Test Values:	
Armature end float:	*0.05 - 0.30 mm (0.002 - 0.12 in.)*
Brush spring tension:	*2.53 - 2.86 lb.*
Commutator, min. diameter:	*33 mm (1.29 in.)*
Brushes, min. length:	*14 mm (0.55 in.)*
Unloaded motor; 12 volts and 40 - 50 amps:	*6,900 - 8,100 rpm*
Loaded motor; 9 volts and 185 - 220 amps:	*1,050 - 1,350 rpm*

12.4.1.   REMOVAL AND INSTALLATION

Remove the negative cable from the battery. Disconnect the leads from the starter motor and take off the starter motor attachment bolts.

Install the starter motor in the reverse sequence to removal and reconnect the motor leads and the battery terminal.

12.4.2. SERVICING

The starter motor and solenoid is shown in Fig. 108. Before dismantling, clean the outside of the motor to remove all grease or dirt. Remember that grease solvents or cleaning fluids should not be allowed to come into contact with the motor or solenoid windings.

Remove the cover from the end of the shaft and take off the "U" lock washer and the adjusting washers. Remove two bolts and take off the end frame. Remove the brush holder. Unscrew the nut holding the field terminal connection and remove the solenoid.

Remove the drive end frame and take out the armature after having removed the shift lever pivot screw. Knock back the stop ring and take out the circlip. Pull off the starter pinion.

Inspect all parts including brushes, commutator, armature shaft and bearings and solenoid contacts. Clean and renovate the commutator as already described for the dynamo. The commutator diameter should not be less than 33 mm (1.30 in.). The insulators between the commutator segments should be undercut to 0.4 mm (0.016 in.) below the surface.

If the armature shaft bushes are to be replaced then note that these are of the oil-retaining type and must be soaked in light oil for at least an hour before fitting.

Replace the brushes and springs if they are worn or weak (see "Technical Data" for details).

When assembling the starter motor, apply grease as follows:

- To the end washers and lock washer.
- To the armature thread and engaging lever groove.
- To the pivot and pins of the shift lever.
- A very thin layer to the solenoid plunger.

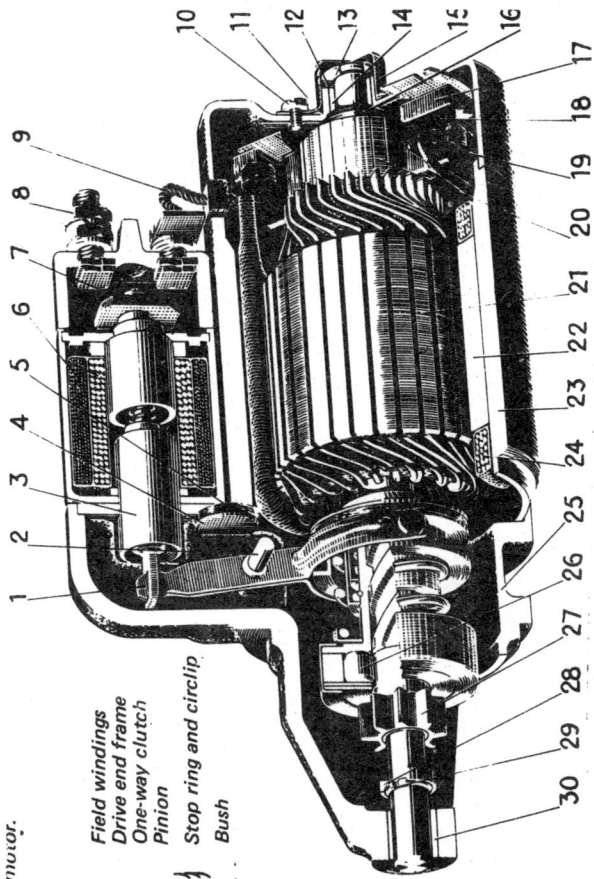

Fig. 108. — Sectional view of the starter motor.

1.
2. } Shift lever and pivot
3. Plunger
4.
5. } Steel and rubber washers
6. Solenoid winding
7. Contact plate
8. Terminal for battery lead
9. Connection to field
10.
11. } Screw and gasket
12.
13. } Shims and circlip
14. Bush
15. Commutator end frame
16. Adjusting washers
17.
18. } Brush holder and brush
19. Brush spring
20. Commutator
21. Armature
22. Pole shoe
23. Stator

24. Field windings
25. Drive end frame
26. One-way clutch
27. Pinion
28.
29. } Stop ring and circlip
30. Bush

Adjust the end float of the armature by means of the end washers. Always replace the stop ring circlip with a new part.

12.5. Fuses

The fuses are contained in a fuse box mounted below the dashboard. There are 12 fuses; three of 8 amp. rating, seven of 5 amp. rating and two of 16 amp. rating.

It is essential that a fuse is always replaced with one of the same rating.

12.6. Bulb Chart

All bulbs are 12 volt.

	Rating	Socket	Number
Headlamps (except 1973)	45/40W	P 45 t	2
Headlamps (1973 models)	60/55W (Halogen type)		
Parking Lights:			
Front:	5W	S 8	2
Rear:	5W (4 cp)	Ba 15 S	2
Flashers, front and rear:	32 cp	Ba 15 S	4
Stop lights	25W (32 cp)	Ba 15 S	2
Reversing lights	15W (32 cp)	Ba 15 S	2
Side markers	5W	Ba 15 S	4
Licence plate (number plate)	5W	S 8	2
Interior light	10W	S 8	1 or 2
Glove compartment	2W	Ba 9 S	1
Instrument lights	2W	W 2.2 d	3
Clock light	2W	Ba 7 S	1
Heater control light	1.2W	W 1.8 d	3
Control panel light	1.2W	W 1.8 d	3
Gear selector light	1.2W	W 1.8 d	1
Warning lamps: charging, turn indicators, parking brake, headlights, oil pressure, rear			

heated window,			
hazard warning,			
overdrive,			
choke: All	*1.2W*	*W 1.8 d*	*1 each*
Warning light,			
model 145,			
rear heated			
window	*2W*	*Ba 7 S*	*1*

13. FUEL INJECTION SYSTEM

13.0. Description

The B20 E and B20 F engines are fitted with an electronically controlled fuel injection system comprising the following units:

— Electronic control unit (under front seat).

— Electric (motor driven) fuel pump (to the right of the fuel tank).

— Fuel filter, pressure regulator, injectors, cold start valve, inlet duct throttle valve switch, auxiliary air regulator, temperature sensor for both induction air and coolant, a pressure sensor in the inlet duct, triggering contacts in the distributor and a thermal timer.

Vehicles fitted with fuel injection and intended for the U.S.A. market are fitted with a gas evaporative control system which prevents gas fumes from being released into the atmosphere.

Vehicles with a B20 F engine and automatic transmission are equipped with exhaust gas recirculation (EGR) to provide cleaner exhaust gases when driving on half throttle.

The fuel injection system is the Bosch type and adjustments and settings are carried out with a special Bosch test instrument and a series of test procedures. It is impossible to check or repair the system without the special equipment and it is recommended that the owner should never interfere with the units or the settings.

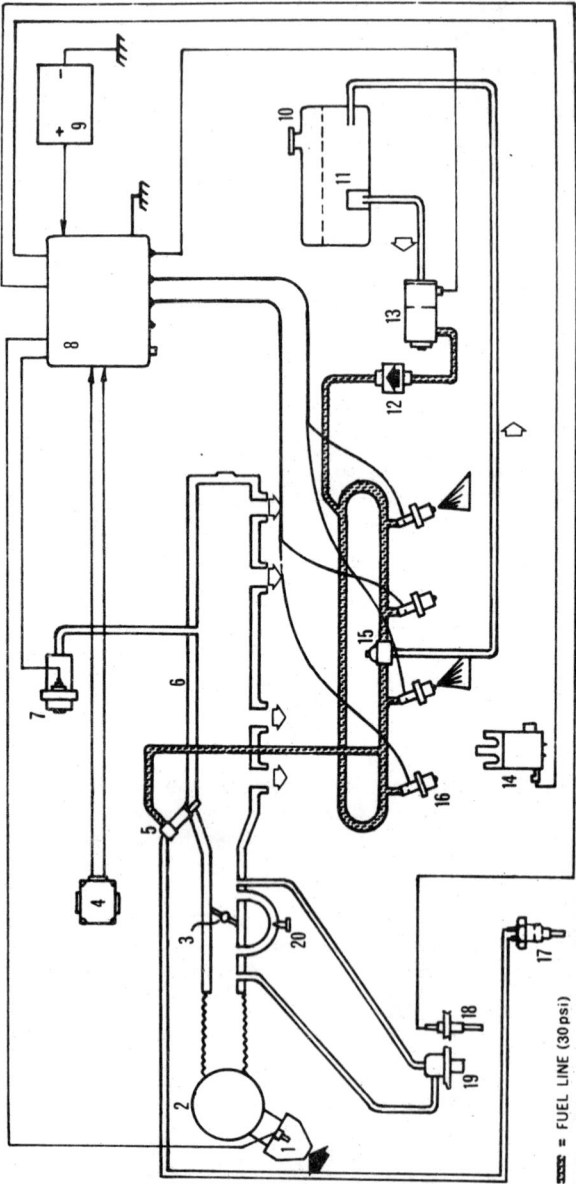

= FUEL LINE (30 psi)

174

Fig. 109. – Schematic diagram of the fuel injection system for the B20 E and F engines.

1. Temperature sensor for induction air
2. Air cleaner
3. Throttle valve
4. Throttle valve switch
5. Cold start valve
6. Inlet duct
7. Pressure sensor (induction air)
8. Control unit
9. Battery
10. Fuel tank
11. Fuel filter, suction line
12. Fuel filter, discharge line
13. Fuel pump
14. Distributor with triggering contacts
15. Pressure regulator
16. Injectors
17. Thermal timer
18. Coolant temperature sensor
19. Auxiliary air regulator
20. Idling adjustment screw

The description of the system unit parts given is for general information only and does not provide sufficient data to enable servicing of the units to be undertaken.

The general principle of the fuel injection system is shown diagrammatically and in a simplified form in Fig. 109.

Fuel is provided by the electric pump, via a fuel filter and fuel line, to the injector circuit. The fuel pressure regulator controls the system pressure to 2.1 kg/sq.cm (30 psi) and a study of the diagram will show that this results in each injector having immediately available a supply of pressurised fuel at the inlet ports.

The electro-magnetic fuel injectors operate in two groups, with 1 and 3 injecting simultaneously and then 2 and 4, the duration of opening being governed basically by engine speed and load.

Before proceeding to a detailed description of the various units it is useful to remember the functions of each which are as follows:

–   The pressure sensor provides information concerning engine load by sensing the absolute pressure at the inlet duct.

–   The triggering contacts in the distributor provide information on the engine speed.

–   The opening time for the cold start valve becomes less with increasing engine temperature and is regulated by the thermal timer relay.

–   The cooling circuit temperature is monitored by the temperature sensor and allows the injectors to remain open a little longer during warm-up of the engine. To cope with this extra flow of fuel the auxiliary air regulator operates, gradually closing as the engine temperature rises.

–   The throttle valve switch monitors the need for additional fuel dependent on the amount and speed of accelerator depression.

13.1. Unit Functions and Descriptions

Control Unit:

The control unit is mounted under the front passenger seat and its function is to process the constant flow of information that is supplied by the various sensors during operation of the engine.

On the right-hand side wheel arch are the main relay for the control unit and the fuel pump control relay.

Fuel Pump:

The fuel pump is of a special design in which the rotor and brush gear are immersed in the fuel. The unit is sealed and cannot be repaired. Fuel is sucked in at the front and discharged at the rear of the pump. The unit is provided with a relief valve opening at 4.5 kg/sq.cm (68 psi) to limit the pressure in the event of a blockage in the fuel system. A check valve closes at 1.2 kg/sq.cm (16 psi) so that the fuel lines will still be under this pressure during the time that the pump is on "stand-by". When the ignition is switched on the pump operates for 1 - 2 seconds and then stops; thereafter, it operates only when the starter motor is engaged or the engine is running.

Fuel Filters:

The system is fitted with two fuel filters; one in the tank for the suction line and one after the pump in the pressure line.

Pressure Regulator:

This unit is mounted between the 2nd and 3rd injectors and is connected to the distributing pipe. The regulator is a mechanical unit and the fuel pressure is set at 2.1 kg/sq.cm (30 psi) by the top adjusting screw and locknut. Once the pressure reaches the required value the valve opens and discharges the excess fuel into the return line.

Injectors:

A section through an injector is shown in Fig. 110 and shows the solenoid which is energised to lift the sealing needle. The valve opening time is variable over the range of 2 - 10 milliseconds to determine the amount of fuel to be injected.

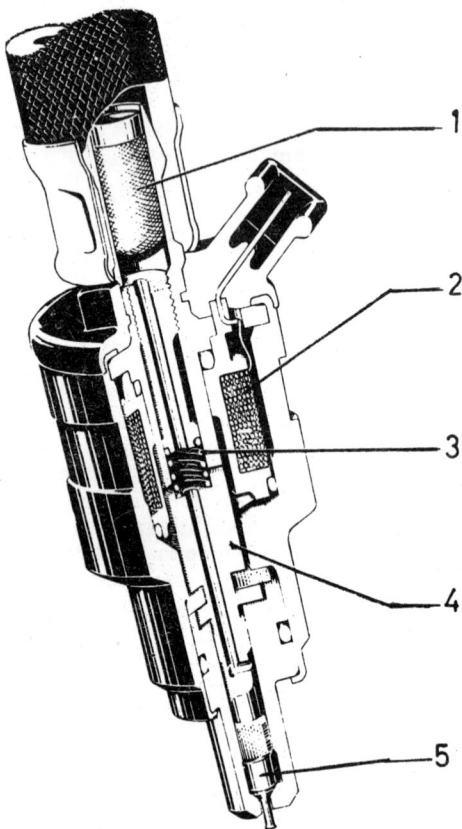

Fig. 110. — Section through the fuel injector.

1. Filter
2. Solenoid coil
3. Return spring
4. Armature
5. Sealing needle

Cold Start Valve:

The cold start valve, mounted in the inlet duct after the throttle, provides extra fuel during the cold start period. The valve will only operate when the starter motor is running and the period of opening is governed by the temperature sensed by the thermal timer.

Thermal Timer:

The thermal timer consists of a bi-metal strip with a resistance heating element. The warming-up time is dependent on the engine operating temperature.

Throttle Valve Switch:

During acceleration periods the switch contacts move across a special zig-zag contact strip arranged in an arc. The number and rapidity of the impulses determine the amount of extra fuel to be injected. During deceleration the switch contacts separate so that impulses are not generated as the accelerator pedal returns.

Pressure Sensor:

The pressure sensor is located on the right-hand wheel housing and connects to the inlet duct by a hose. The sensor contains an aneroid capsule that senses the absolute pressure in the inlet duct. This is another way of saying that the sensor is not simply acting on the inlet pressure but is also comparing this with the atmospheric pressure as well. It is this feature that ensures that the engine requirements are correctly met no matter if the vehicle is at sea level or a higher altitude.

Auxiliary Air Regulator:

This unit is placed so that it is in contact with the coolant system and thus able to admit more air to the duct at cold start and during the warm-up period.

Temperature Sensors:

The system includes two sensors, one for the coolant and one for the intake air. Low temperatures measured by either of these units will result in an increase in injection time. The coolant sensor, therefore, has a different function to the auxiliary air regulator.

Triggering Contacts:

The distributor for fuel injection includes a secondary cam and a pair of triggering contacts to supply the control unit with information concerning the engine speed and thus enable the commencement and duration of injection to be controlled in conjunction with the information from the pressure sensor.

13.2. Fuel Injection -- Special Instructions

Vehicles fitted with fuel injection are subject to the following restrictions which must always be observed:

— NEVER let the engine run with the battery disconnected.

— DO NOT use a rapid battery charger as an aid to starting. Disconnect at least one battery lead before using a rapid battery charger.

— DO NOT disconnect any part of the control unit with the ignition switched on.

— The fuel pump is polarity-sensitive and must only be connected in accordance with the markings on the casing.

— GREAT CARE must be taken to exclude all dirt or contamination from the fuel system and the injectors.

— DO NOT allow the control unit to be exposed to temperatures above 185° F (stove painting in an oven for example). Remove the unit first and tow the vehicle in and out.

— NEVER apply battery voltage to the injector terminals to test.

13.3. Servicing

Experience has shown that the electronic fuel injection system should run for around 100,000 km (60,000 miles) without the need for replacements or adjustments.

The only attention necessary is to change and clean the fuel filters. Note that the pressure line filter must be fitted with the arrow pointing in the direction of fuel flow.

For the gas evaporative control system, the plastic foam filter (at the bottom of the venting filter) should be replaced after 40,000 km (24,000 miles). The exhaust gas recirculation valve requires no routine maintenance and cannot be dismantled.

FAULT FINDING SECTION

The following section lists some of the more common faults that can develop in a motor car. The section is divided in various categories and it should be possible to locate faults or damage by referring to the assembly group of the vehicle in question.

The faults are listed in no particular order and their causes are given a number. By referring to this number it is possible to read off the possible cause and to carry out the necessary remedies, if this is within the scope of your facilities.

ENGINE FAULTS

Engine will not crank:	1, 2, 3, 4
Engine cranks, but will not start:	5, 6, 7, 8
Engine cranks very slowly:	1, 2, 3
Engine starts, but cuts out:	5, 6, 9, 10
Engines misfires in the lower speed ranges:	5, 6, 9, 11
Engine misfires in the higher speed ranges:	5, 6, 11, 12
Continuous misfiring:	5, 6, 7, 10 to 15, 21, 22
Max. revs. not obtained:	5, 6, 9, 12, 22
Faulty idling:	5, 6, 8 to 11, 13, 15, 16, 21 and 22
Lack of power:	3, 5 to 11, 13 to 15, 22
Lack of acceleration:	5 to 8, 12, 14 to 16
Lack of max. speed:	5 to 8, 10, 12, 13 to 15, 22
Excessive fuel consumption:	3, 5, 6, 15, 16
Excessive oil consumption:	16 to 19
Pinking and running-on (dieseling)	5, 6
Low compression:	7, 11 to 13, 16, 20 to 22

CAUSES AND REMEDIES

1. Fault in the starter motor or its connections. Refer to "Electrical Faults".

2. Engine oil too thick. This can be caused by using the wrong oil, low temperatures or using oil not suitable for the prevailing climates. Depress the

clutch whilst starting. Otherwise refill the engine with the correct oil grade.

3.	Moveable parts of engine not run-in. This fault may be noticed when the engine has been overhauled. It may be possible to free the engine by adding oil to the fuel for a while.

4.	Mechanical fault. This may be due to seizure of the piston(s), broken crankshaft, connecting rods, clutch or other moveable parts of the engine. The engine must be stripped for inspection.

5.	Fault in the ignition system. Refer to "Ignition Faults".

6.	Fault in the fuel system. Refer to "Fuel Faults".

7.	Incorrect valve timing. This will only be noticed after the engine has been re-assembled after overhaul. Re-dismantle and check the timing marks on the timing gear wheels.

8.	Compression leak due to faulty closing of valves. Check valve clearances. See also under (7.) or leakage past worn piston rings or pistons. Cylinder head gasket blown.

9.	Entry of air at inlet manifold, due to split manifold or damaged gasket. Correct as necessary.

10.	Restriction in exhaust system, due to damaged exhaust pipes, dirt in end of pipe, kinked pipes, or collapsed silencer. Repair as necessary.

11.	Worn valves or valve seats, no longer closing the valves properly. Top overhaul of engine is asked for.

12.	Sticking valves due to excessive carbon deposits or weak valve springs. Top overhaul is asked for.

13.	Cylinder head gasket blown. Replace gasket and check block and head surfaces for distortion.

14.	Camshaft worn, not opening or closing one of the valves properly, preventing proper combustion. Check and if necessary fit new camshaft.

15.	Incorrect valve (tappet) clearance. Re-adjust.

16.	Cylinder bores, piston or piston rings worn. Overhaul is the only cure. Fault may be corrected for a while by adding "Piston Seal Liquid" into the cylinders, but will re-develop.

17. Worn valve guides and/or valve stems. Top overhaul is asked for.

18. Damaged valve stem seals. Top overhaul is asked for.

19. Leaking crankshaft oil seal, worn piston rings or pistons, worn cylinders. Correct as necessary.

20. Loose spark plug, gases escaping past threads, or plug sealing washer damaged. Correct.

21. Cracked cylinder or cylinder block. Dismantle, investigate and replace block if necessary.

22. Broken, weak or collapsed valve spring(s). Top overhaul is asked for.

IGNITION FAULTS

Engine does not start:	1 to 3, 5, 6, 8 to 14, 19
Engine misfires:	2 to 7, 9 to 12, 14, 19
One cylinder not working:	2 to 7, 9 to 14
Engine fails to rev, misfires on acceleration:	2 to 7, 9 to 12, 14, 19
Incorrect idling speed:	1 to 3, 5 to 15, 17
Lack of power:	2 to 12, 14, 15, 17, 19
Poor acceleration:	As for "Lack of Power"
Lack of max. speed:	As for "Lack of Power"
Excessive fuel consumption:	As for "Lack of Power"
Pinking and running-on (dieseling):	2, 3, 5, 6, 8, 11, 12, 15, 16, 18

CAUSES AND REMEDIES

1. Battery discharged or defective. Try charging the battery or replace. Use slave battery to start the engine.

2. Contact breakers not working properly. Clean old points or replace.

3. Contact breakers connected to earth. This could happen after replacement of the points.

4. Contact breaker arm spring too weak. Check with spring scale. Renew points if necessary.

5. Spark plugs need attention. Check condition of plug faces, clean plugs and adjust electrode gaps to specification. Check when plugs have been replaced last time.

6. Incorrect spark plug gaps. See also under 5.

7. Wrong type of spark plug fitted. Check with the specifications and install correct plugs.

8. Ignition timing not correctly adjusted. Check and re-time ignition if necessary, using a stroboscopic timing lamp if possible.

9. Coil or condensor defective. No repairs possible, replace, making sure that condensor with correct mfd value is fitted.

10. Loose connection in L.T. circuit (small lead at side of distributor for example). Check and correct.

11. Open circuit, short circuit to ground (earth) or centre lead of coil not fitted properly. Check all cables and make sure centre lead makes contact.

12. The same as 11, but fault is in the spark plug leads. Check for broken cables and proper connections.

13. Plug leads incorrectly connected. Fault only evident after distributor or plugs have been removed and leads incorrectly connected. Follow firing order and reconnect properly.

14. "Tracking" present. This means that H.T. voltage is creeping to ground (earth) due to dirt, or or dampness. Various products (damp start) are available to overcome problem, mainly if caused by dampness (water spray, rain, etc.).

15. Centrifugal advance not operating properly. Check by removing distributor cap, turn rotor against tension of flyweight springs and release. Rotor should return to original position (no sticking).

16. Vacuum advance not operating. Pull off vacuum hose at distributor with engine running and then re-connect. Engine noise must change if engine speed is increased.

17. Distributor cam or shaft worn. Overhaul distributor or fit replacement unit (correct one).

18. Fuel with incorrect octane rating used. Check with

manufacturers recommendation.
Pinking can also be caused by overheating of the engine or too much advanced ignition timing.

19. Carbon brush in distributor cap worn or spring too weak. Check and replace if necessary.

LUBRICATION SYSTEM FAULTS

The only problem the lubrication system should give is excessive oil consumption or low oil pressure, or the oil warning light not going off.

Excessive oil consumption can be caused by worn cylinder bores, pistons and/or piston rings, worn valve guides, worn valve stem seals or a damaged crankshaft oil seal or leaking gasket on any of the engine parts. In most cases the engine must be dismantled to locate the fault.

Low oil pressure can be caused by a faulty oil pressure gauge, sender unit or wiring, a defective relief valve, low oil level, blocked oil pick-up pipe for the oil pump, worn oil pump or damaged main or big end bearings. In most cases it is logical to check the oil level first and then the operation of the oil pressure gauge. All other causes require the dismantling and repair of the engine.

If the oil warning light stays on (if fitted), switch off the engine IMMEDIATELY, as delay could cause complete seizure of the engine within minutes.

COOLING SYSTEM FAULTS (water-cooled engines only)

Common faults are: Overheating, loss of coolant and slow warming up of the engine:

Overheating:

1. Lack of coolant: Open the radiator cap with care to avoid injuries. Never pour cold water into an overheated engine. Wait until engine cools down and pour in coolant whilst engine is running.

2. Radiator core obstructed by leaves, insects, etc.: Blow with air line from the back of the radiator or with the water hose to clean.

3. Fan belt loose or slipping: Re-adjust fan belt tension or replace. In emergency use a nylon stocking to make up a make-shift fan belt by tieing the stocking around all pulleys.

4. Thermostat sticking: If sticking in the closed position, coolant can only circulate within the cylinder block. Remove thermostat and check as described in Section "Cooling".

5. Water hose split: Identified by rising steam from the engine compartment. Slight splits can be repaired with insulation tape. Drive without radiator cap to keep the pressure in the system down, to the nearest service station.

6. Ignition or carburettor incorrectly adjusted: Adjust accordingly.

7. Water pump inoperative: Overhaul or replace water pump.

8. Cylinder head gasket blown: Replace the cylinder head gasket.

Loss of Coolant:

1. Radiator leaks: Slight leaks may be stopped by using radiator sealing compound (follow the instructions of the manufacturer). In emergency a raw egg can be cracked open and poured into the radiator filler neck.

2. Hose leaks: See under 5, "Overheating".

3. Water pump leaks: Check the gasket for proper sealing or overhaul (replace) the pump.

Long Warming-up Periods:

1. Thermostat sticking in the open position: Remove thermostat, check and if necessary replace.

FUEL SYSTEM FAULTS

Engine does not start:	1 to 8
Engine starts, but stops soon afterwards:	1, 3 to 6, 8 to 13, 18, 19
Engine misfires low revs.:	3, 4, 8, 9
Engine misfires at high revs.:	1, 3, 4, 8, 9
Engine misfires continuously:	1 to 6, 8, 9, 12 to 14
Engine fails to rev:	1, 3, 4, 8, 9, 11 to 17, 21
Bad idling:	4, 8 to 14, 18, 19, 21
Lack of power:	4, 8, 11 to 14, 19, 21

Lack of max. speed:	4, 8, 11 to 15, 17, 19, 21
Excessive fuel consumption:	3, 4, 11, 12, 16, 17, 19, 21
Pinking:	15, 20, 21
Backfiring:	4, 9, 11, 13, 14,

CAUSES AND REMEDIES

1. Fuel tank empty. Refuel.

2. Fuel line or pipe blocked. Remove pipes and blow through it with compressed air to remove obstruction.

3. Fuel pump not operating. Remove pump and check operation. Repair or replace.

4. Carburettor jets blocked (if applicable). Remove all jets and blow through them with compressed air or in emergency with the mouth.

5. Air lock in fuel pipe. Unscrew pipe and blow through it with compressed air.

6. Fuel filter blocked. Remove filter from its location and clean or replace.

7. Float chamber needle valve sticking. Unscrew float chamber cover, remove needle valve and free off or replace valve. Fit cover with new gasket.

8. Water in carburettor. Clean out float chamber and all jets.

9. Restricted fuel flow due to foreign body in fuel supply lines. Clean out lines.

10. Slow-running speed too low. Adjust to proper value.

11. Choke control improperly adjusted. Adjust in the case of manual choke and check setting in the case of automatic choke.

12. Float level out of adjustment. Adjust in accordance with instructions in Section "Fuel System".

13. Carburettor icing up. Very rare fault on modern carburettors. Engine will restart after the ice has thawed up.

14. Inlet manifold sucks in additional air. Check all gaskets on manifold and replace if necessary.

15. Fuel with incorrect octane rating used. Use proper fuel grade. Check with manufacturer.

16. Accelerator pump not operating. Dismantle carburettor and check linkage, lever and diaphragm.

17. Throttle operating linkage wrongly adjusted. Check and adjust as necessary.

18. Slow-running mixture not adjusted properly. Readjust slow-running speed in accordance with instructions in Section "Fuel System".

19. Air filter element obstructed. Remove element and check. Replace if due for renewal.

20. Ignition timing incorrectly adjusted. Adjust in accordance with instructions in Section "Ignition System".

21. Incorrect carburettor jets fitted. Applies not to fixed jet carburettors. Check with setting table in Section "Fuel System".

CLUTCH FAULTS

Clutch slipping:	1, 2, 3, 4, 5
Clutch will not disengage fully:	4, 6 to 12, 14
Clutch judder:	1, 2, 7, 10 to 13
Whining from clutch when pedal is depressed:	13
Clutch noise when idling:	2, 3
Clutch noise during engagement:	2

CAUSES AND REMEDIES

1. Insufficient clutch free play at pedal. Adjust in accordance with instructions in Section "Clutch".

2. Clutch disc linings worn, hardened, oiled-up, loose or broken. Disc distorted or hub loose. Clutch disc must be replaced.

3. Pressure plate fault. Replace clutch.

4.* Air in hydraulic system (only applicable to models with hydraulic clutch control). Low fluid level in clutch cylinder reservoir.

5. Insufficient play at clutch pedal and clutch release linkage (the latter in the case of mechanical clutch operation). Adjust as described.

6. Excessive free play in release linkage (only for cable and linkage operated clutch). Adjust or replace worn parts.

7. Misalignment of clutch housing. Very rare fault, but possible on transmissions with separate clutch housings. Re-align to correct.

8. Clutch disc hub binding on splines of main drive shaft (clutch shaft) due to dirt or burrs on splines. Remove clutch and clean and check splines.

9. Clutch disc linings loose or broken. Replace disc.

10. Pressure plate distorted. Replace clutch.

11. Clutch cover distorted. Replace clutch.

12. Fault in transmission or loose engine mountings.

13. Release bearing defective. Remove clutch and replace bearing.

14. Bend clutch release lever. Check lever and replace or straighten if possible.

* The above faults and remedies are for hydraulic and mechanical clutch operation and should be read as applicable to the model in question, as the clutch fault finding section is written for all types of clutch operation.

STEERING FAULTS

Steering very heavy:	1 to 6
Steering very loose:	5, 7 to 9, 11 to 13
Steering wheel wobbles:	4, 5, 7 to 9, 11 to 16
Vehicle pulls to one side:	1, 4, 8, 10, 14 to 18
Steering wheel doe not return to centre pos.:	1 to 6, 18
Abnormal tyre wear:	1, 4, 7 to 9, 14 to 19
Knocking noise in column:	6, 7, 11, 12,

CAUSES AND REMEDIES

1. Tyre pressures not correct or uneven. Correct.

2. Low oil level in steering gear (if steering is filled with oil). Otherwise lack of lubricant on rack and pinion steering.

3. Stiff steering linkage ball joints. Re-grease if provisions are made for it, otherwise replace ball joints in question.

4. Incorrect wheel alignment. Correct as necessary.

5. Steering needs adjustment. Adjust as necessary.

6. Steering column bearings too tight or seized or steering column bent. Correct as necessary.

7. Steering linkage joints loose or worn. Check and replace joints as necessary.

8. Front wheel bearings worn, damaged or loose. Re-adjust bearing play or replace the bearings if no result can be obtained.

9. Front suspension parts loose. Check and correct.

10. Wheel nuts loose. Re-tighten.

11. Steering wheel loose. Re-tighten nut.

12. Steering gear mounting loose. Check and tighten.

13. Steering gear worn. Although it may be possible to overhaul the steering, the fitting of a replacement steering could be the solution.

14. Steering damper (if fitted) defective or loose.

15. Wheels not properly balanced or tyre pressures uneven. Correct pressures or balance wheels.

16. Suspension springs weak or broken. Replace spring in question or both.

17. Brakes are pulling to one side. See under "Brake Faults".

18. Suspension out of alignment. Have the complete suspension checked by a dealer.

19. Improper driving. We don't intend to tell you how to drive and are quite sure that this is not the cause of the fault.

BRAKE FAULTS

Brake Failure: Brake shoe linings or pads excessively worn, incorrect brake fluid (after overhaul), insufficient brake fluid, fluid leak, master cylinder defective, wheel cylinder or caliper failure. Remedies are obvious in each instance.

Brakes Ineffective: Shoe linings or pads worn, incorrect lining material or brake fluid, linings contaminated, fluid level low, air in brake system (bleed brakes), leak in pipes or cylinders, master cylinder defective. Remedies are obvious in each instance.

Brakes pull to one side: Shoes or linings worn, incorrect linings or pads, contaminated linings, drums or discs scored, fluid pipe blocked, unequal tyre pressures, brake back plate or caliper mounting loose, wheel bearings not properly adjusted, brakes need adjustment, wheel cylinder seized. Remedy as necessary.

Brake pedal spongy: Air in hydraulic system, System must be bled of air.

Pedal travel too far: Linings or pads worn, brakes need adjustment, drums or discs scored, master cylinder or wheel cylinders defective, system needs bleeding. Rectify as necessary.

Loss of brake pressure: Fluid leak, air in system, leak in master or wheel cylinders, brake servo not operating (vacuum hose disconnected from inlet manifold — if a brake servo is fitted). Place vehicle on dry ground and depress brake pedal. Check where fluid runs out and rectify as necessary.

Brakes binding: Incorrect brake fluid (boiling), weak shoe return springs, brakes adjusted improperly, piston in caliper or wheel cylinder seized, push rod play on master cylinder insufficient (compensation port obstructed), handbrake adjusted too tightly. Rectify as necessary. Swelling of cylinder cups through use of incorrect fluid could be another reason.

Handbrake ineffective: Brake shoe linings worn, linings contaminated, operating lever on brake shoe seized, brake shoes or handbrake need adjusting. Rectify as necessary.

Excessive pedal pressure required: Brake shoe linings or brake pads worn, linings or pads contaminated, brake servo vacuum hose disconnected from manifold, master or wheel brake cylinder seized. Rectify as necessary.

Brakes squealing: Brake shoe linings or pads worn so far that metal is grinding against drum or disc. Inside of drum is full of lining dust. Remove and replace, or clean out the drum(s).

ELECTRICAL FAULTS

Starter motor failure:	2 to 5, 8, 9
No starter motor drive:	1 to 3, 5 to 7
Slow cranking speed:	1 to 3
Charge warning light remains on:	3, 10 to 12
Charge warning light does not come on:	2, 3, 9, 11, 13
Headlamp failure:	2, 3, 11, 13, 15 to 17
Battery needs frequent topping-up:	11
Direction indicators not operating:	2, 3, 9, 13, 15, 18
Battery frequently discharged	3, 10, 11, 12,

CAUSES AND REMEDIES

1. Tight engine. Check and rectify.

2. Battery discharged or defective. Re-charge battery or replace if older than approx. 2 years.

3. Interrupted connection in circuit. Trace and rectify.

4. Starter motor pinion jammed in flywheel. Release.

5. Also 6, 7 and 8. Starter motor defective, no engagement in flywheel, pinion or flywheel worn or solenoid switch defective. Correct as necessary.

9. Ignition/starter switch inoperative. Replace.

10. Drive belt loose or broken. Adjust or replace.

11. Regulator defective. Adjust or replace.

12. Generator inoperative. Overhaul or replace.

13. Bulb burnt out. Replace.
15. Flasher unit defective. Replace.